Fundamentals of Crisis
Counseling

Fundamentals of Crisis Counseling

William Getz
University of Washington

Allen E. Wiesen

Stan Sue
University of Washington

Amy Ayers
Overlake Memorial Hospital

Lexington Books
D.C. Heath and Company
Lexington, Massachusetts
Toronto   London

Library of Congress Cataloging in Publication Data

Main entry under title:

Fundamentals of crisis counseling.

    1. Crisis intervention (Psychiatry) I. Getz, William.
RC480.5.F86   362.2'2   73-15925
ISBN 0-669-91173-9

Second Printing, July 1977

Published simultaneously in Canada.

Printed in the United States of America.

International Standard Book Number: 0-669-91173-9

Library of Congress Catalog Card Number: 73-15925

TO THE C.C.'s

Reuben	Karen	Kim R.	Cindy
Eric	Saul	Sue	Greg
Ely	Dave	Sara	Leanne
Richard	Keith	Al	Kim W.
Ellen	Marsha	Carol M.	Lee
Bill	Norm	Diane	Michell
Mike	Beth	Linda	Barb Z.
Brett	Jan	Marty	Dennis
Barry	Barbie	Barb S.	Diane R.
Ed	Gary	Evalyn	Lois
Byron	Chris	Kay	Beverly
Don	Ruth	Marge	Gordon
Carol H.	Candy	Judy	Alice
Marianna	Jim	Gert	Roy
Dorothy	Juanita	Nancy	Damaris

Contents

List of Figures

Introduction

The fundamentals of crisis counseling are not merely mechanical steps for dealing with severe personal crisis, but are a blending of humanistic guidelines and practical knowledge to make the crisis encounter a growth experience. The function of the crisis counselor is to help the person in distress to develop and enhance his capacity to meet successfully future crises, to grow rather than regress in his collision with reality.

To this end we have attempted to provide the counselor in training as well as the experienced practitioner with both a sound conceptual background in crisis work and specific guidelines in promoting the client's growth in crisis.

In Part I, we have drawn heavily upon well-established principles of human behavior to familiarize the reader with the essential social science background of crisis work. But we have gone beyond this in Part II by providing specific applications of these principles in actual case histories. Thus the reader is able to compare his approach to those that have proven effective in our own work. This integration of theory with direct application is one of the innovative features of this book.

It is essential to note that crisis counseling is just one facet of psychotherapy. It is not intended to be used in all cases nor in all situations, but only those in which there is an element of immediate crisis. Thus, for example, a long-term case of moderate anxiety with no newly emerging developments would not be suitable for crisis intervention. Nor, on the other hand, would crisis counseling be appropriate for treating deeply ingrained, long-standing psychological and social problems. Nevertheless, crisis work has its unique place in psychotherapy, often being the treatment of choice over other approaches. It is not a "second-class citizen" but a fully accredited mode of therapeutically altering human behavior. With crisis counseling then, as with all other modes of psychotherapy, the clinician must be able to make the critical judgment as to when to use it.

Throughout this book we have focused upon the individual in crisis. However, most, if not all, the principles we have offered have immediate and general application to families and other intimate groups. Specifically, the crisis counselor will find the deductive method as described in Part I, indispensable in working with any unit—the individual, the couple, the family, the small group—which presents a crisis.

A brief Appendix includes essential information for anyone practicing crisis counseling.

In Part II we have assembled several case histories taken from actual transcripts with persons in crisis. We urge the reader to become deeply involved in these case histories rather than merely dealing with them in the abstract. They can provide the counselor with valuable indirect experience. It is our firm belief that serious study of this book will enable the crisis worker to attain knowledge and skills that will greatly improve his competence in assisting the person in crisis to meet, overcome, and grow from his conflict.

We wish to express our gratitude to Mr. Ken Grace, formerly of the Eastside Community Mental Health Center and Mr. Bob Rabideau of Overlake Hospital for their support in this endeavor. Similar thanks are expressed to Drs. Keith Tucker, Charles Martin, Harold Weeks, Jack Leversee, of Overlake Hospital, and Dr. Ed Bigler, of Valley General Hospital.

Numerous persons offered critical comments and lent support to us at important times: Gene Stein, Bert Goldberg, Ned Wagner, Lee Anderson, Herb Steger, Irwin Sarason, Bob Campbell, Betty Hopper, Bill Moyer, James Straughn, Keith Crnic—to name a few.

We wish also to thank Mrs. Gale Mowrer for typing the manuscript.

William L. Getz

Part I

1

The Historical Development of Crisis Intervention

All human beings inevitably face stress situations during their lives. The death of a loved one, divorce, loss of a job, or entrance into school may produce marked emotional reactions. The person is then called upon to adapt to these life changes and to deal with the accompanying emotional states. A crisis develops when an individual is under intense stress and cannot readily resolve the situation by using previously employed coping mechanisms. Yet a crisis state offers two divergent possibilities: increased personal growth and adjustment, or further disorganization and maladjustment (Aguilera, Messick, Farrell 1970).

Crisis intervention techniques can help an individual resolve personal disorganization and emotional turmoil. Although they have been formally delineated only in recent years, it is obvious that provisions for helping individuals in stress situations have been present in every society throughout man's existence. Witch doctors and shamans were often called upon by tribesmen to resolve personal or tribal problems. Similarly, the help of friends, relatives, priests, doctors, and teachers has traditionally been enlisted by persons experiencing crisis. The typical intervention method included expressions of sympathy and support, or even appeals to a deity. The assumption was that with proper guidance and understanding, the person could mobilize inner strengths to overcome or to adjust to the situation.

Two particularly important events helped to shape the development of current forms of crisis intervention techniques. First, traditional forms of psychotherapy were found to be inappropriate. Most, like psychoanalysis, were geared to major personality and behavior change. Thus, a different type of intervention, one focusing on clients in crisis, had to be found. Second, there was growing recognition that certain situations tended to precipitate crisis, and that persons experiencing crisis frequently reacted in somewhat predictable patterns. This led to both the study of crisis and to the development of intervention techniques specifically designed to deal with the person in crisis.

Classical Psychoanalysis:
Theory and Practice

Crisis intervention was influenced by a number of therapeutic approaches, all concerned directly or indirectly with behavior change. Let us first examine briefly some of the concepts of Sigmund Freud, whose theories have had a profound influence upon psychological thought. Freudian, or classical, psycho-analysis was essentially developed to treat neurotic clients rather than individuals in immediate crisis. However, as a basis for comparing modern crisis intervention with a traditional mode of psychotherapy, it is useful to review key Freudian concepts.

Id, Ego, Superego

Freud attempted to relate his theory of personality development to his psychoanalytic treatment technique. The notions of intrapsychic conflicts, psychic determinism, and psychosexual states are fundamental to his theory. According to Freud, man is born with life instincts (*Eros*), which represent all of the constructive survival tendencies such as hunger, thirst, and sex. In addition, there are also death instincts (*Thanatos*), from which the aggressive drives derive. The instincts impel behavior and constantly seek expression. From a Freudian viewpoint, the *id* is an unconscious, biological, and instinctual aspect of the human personality. The id seeks to reduce immediately any tension or need that arises and is not constrained by objective reality. It follows the pleasure principle, seeking direct gratification.

Since the subjective, irrational, lustful, and sometimes self-destructive demands of the id frequently conflict with the limitations imposed by society, Freud posited the *superego* as that part of the personality that represented the values and ideals of the society as expressed through the parents. It acted as the moral arm, concerned with right and wrong and perfection. The superego often inhibited the id from unrestrained expression of impulses, particularly the sexual or aggressive ones, since the direct expression of these was condemned by society. Pressure was also placed upon the ego, the mediator between the person and reality, to find morally acceptable means of satisfying needs. The superego was composed of the conscience (making the individual feel guilty for wrong-doings) and the ego ideal (making the individual feel proud for achieving well).

Finally, Freud conceptualized the *ego* as the rational, reality-oriented executive part of the individual. It functions to reduce organismic tension within the limits of reality and the environment. Complete and unrestrained expression of id demands was not possible if the individual was to function safely in society. The ego, then, served to mediate between the id demands and the conditions of the environment.

Psychological disorders occurred because the id, ego, and superego were in conflict with one another. The ego and superego had to constrain the irrational impulses of the id, while the ego and superego themselves often clashed. These conflicts resulted in the use of defense mechanisms such as repression, regression, fixation, and reaction formation. Repression was the basic defense mechanism and served to bar from consciousness id impulses that threatened to be upsetting to the individual. Behavior, whether normal or disordered, was an indirect expression of the id, ego, and/or superego forces and their conflicts. Thus, dreams, slips of the tongue, errors, and forgetting were all psychically determined, and though they seemed trivial to most, Freud felt they had purpose and meaning.

The psychosexual development also played an important role in disorders. The individual, according to Freud, expresses his sexuality from infancy, though the sexuality is expressed at first not via the genitals, but through oral and, later, anal activities. A conflict, such as lack of oral gratification or, later on, a difficult time during toilet training, may lead to a *fixation* at a particular stage. Such a fixation reduces the amount of energy available to the ego, thus reducing the individual's ability to cope with reality. The more energy diverted to conflicts, the less available for the development of the genital stage (preceded by phallic and less significant latency periods), and the less complete the individual's psychosexual development. Adult problems then, were often viewed as symptomatic of, or at least influenced by, the particular stage at which the individual was still fixated.

Freud's method of therapy was closely related to his theory of disordered behavior. Free association, dream analysis, interpretations, catharsis, and transference were important processes in the therapeutic relationship. Since many of the client's anxiety-producing instinctual urges and conflicts were repressed from consciousness, the task of the psychoanalyst was to uncover unconscious material in an unthreatening and nondirective manner so that the client's ego could gain insight and bring instinctual impulses into more adequate ego control. By free associating (freely speaking about anything that came to mind) and recounting dreams, the client gave clues as to the nature of the unresolved conflicts, which the analyst then interpreted back to the client. It was assumed that free association and the recollection of dreams were nonthreatening and yet meaningful activities. Throughout the therapeutic process, the analyst would be alert for *resistances* on the part of the client, impediments to therapy owing to unconscious resistance. Again, resistances were indicative of the client's problems and also represented an opportunity for the analyst to provide feedback to the client.

At times, it might be appropriate for the client to experience *catharsis*, a release of emotions that had previously not been given adequate expression. One very important emotional reaction that Freud noticed was called *transference*. Clients often reacted toward the analyst in emotionally inappropriate ways, that is, in ways that were not elicited by the analyst. For example, the client might express a great deal of hostility or affection toward the analyst, who had done nothing to provoke these feelings. These inappropriate or unjustified emotions were interpreted by the analyst as symptoms of the client's early childhood conflicts. They revealed information about prior reactions to parental figures or other significant persons. These reactions, too, could be used to help the client gain insight and understanding into his behavior.

In summary, classical Freudian therapy stemmed from his theory of personality. The analyst had to assess the client's behaviors. These were presumed to be symptomatic of early childhood conflicts involving the id, ego, and superego. By appropriately interpreting these behaviors back to the client, the analyst tried to facilitate better conscious control of unresolved conflicts by the client.

Psychoanalysis and Crisis Intervention

Undoubtedly, classical psychoanalysis has had a major impact on our thinking regarding deviant behavior and psychotherapeutic treatment. It has, however, experienced severe criticism on numerous grounds. Many psychoanalysts (Adler, Jung, and Sullivan) disagreed with Freud in regard to theory of a basic biological drive. As a result, variations of Freudian psychoanalysis developed (Erikson 1950; Horney 1939; Fromm 1955; Alexander and French 1946). Some individuals found psychoanalytic theory and its concepts to be difficult to test or validate (Ellis 1950), and others have criticized psychoanalysis for not demonstrating effectiveness in the treatment of disorders (Eysenck 1952). It is beyond the scope of this book to deal with these criticisms. Rather, our intention is to evaluate the applicability of psychoanalysis to the individual experiencing a crisis.

There are many practical problems inherent in psychoanalysis that reduce its effectiveness as a preferred treatment approach for crisis clients. Because its aim is to affect major personality change, classical psychoanalysis is usually a long-term, intensive experience. If we assume that crises are quite common and that many individuals need treatment, then it becomes a practical problem of supplying enough analysts for clients. The supply and demand issue is critical since crisis clients need immediate attention and aid (Jacobson, Wilner, Morley, Schneider, Strickler, and Sommer 1965). Furthermore, many clients have neither the time nor the financial resources to engage in psychoanalysis. There are other limitations. Some clients prove to be difficult to work with in psychoanalytic treatment. Fenichel indicated that certain client characteristics might be contraindicated for this type of treatment (1945). These include age (being too young or too old), disturbances of speech, lack of a reasonable and cooperative ego, a schizoid personality, and an urgent neurotic symptom. Because it was apparent that other forms of therapy also posed similar problems, clinicians began to realize that in order to meet the needs of crisis clients, a different type of therapy had to be developed. This realization, coupled with the study of the crisis state, led to current crisis intervention techniques.

Regardless of his therapeutic approach, a therapist often encounters clients in crisis. In such cases, the therapist may utilize the techniques appropriate to his mode of therapy. Although we have so far compared only one mode of treatment, psychoanalysis, with crisis intervention, it seems necessary to mention briefly other forms of therapy and their possible application to crisis clients.

Client-Centered Therapy

In contrast to the Freudian approach, client-centered, Gestalt, and behavior therapies focus primarily on the here and now. Discussions of the client's past experiences and recollections are kept to a minimum, except where they have direct relevance to the present situation. In *client-centered therapy*, man is assumed to be basically good, rational, and striving for positive growth. However, growth is hampered by threats to one's self-concept. As an individual grows older, he learns to incorporate certain attributes that define him as a worthy individual. These attributes, because they are derived from the values of significant others, may result in an unrealistic self-concept. Experiences that are at odds with one's self-concept are threatening and lead to defenses and maladjustment. In order to facilitate growth in the client, the therapist assumes the attitude of unconditional positive regard toward the client. By valuing and helping to clarify the client's feelings, the therapist facilitates the client's self-acceptance. Since it is the client who must grow and decide for himself, the therapist generally avoids giving advice, exhortations or in-depth interpretations. (Rogers 1951).

Gestalt Therapy

Gestalt therapy assumes that man often experiences unresolved conflicts (as in Freudian theory). These conflicts cause tension and reduce one's energy for self growth. Frequently, the individual blocks out the conflicts and the feelings from awareness. But since the conflicts still exist in the form of "unfinished business," the individual engages in repetitious behaviors, game playing, and rigidity in order to avoid confronting them. The task of the Gestalt therapist is to help the client develop awareness of self and the world. The individual is encouraged to attend to his perceptions and bodily sensations, to talk about how he feels but not why. The client is often asked to confront conflicts, to note discrepancies between words and behaviors, to act out fantasies, and to role-play. Rather than being objective and detached, the therapist regards therapy as an encounter in which both the client and counselor become deeply involved. The emphasis is on the process of getting in touch with one's self rather than on the outcome. (Perls, Hefferline, Goodman 1965).

Behavior Modification Techniques

Behavior therapy is based upon the assumption that maladaptive behaviors are learned and maintained in accordance with the principles of conditioning (Wolpe 1969; Bandura 1969). In the same way that these behaviors were learned, they can be unlearned or modified by utilizing learning principles with the client and his environment. Extinction, counterconditioning, rewards, aversive conditioning, desensitization, and modeling have been successfully used to change behavior. Although relatively little has been written about behavior modification approaches with crisis clients, some analysis has been made of depression and suicidal behaviors (Lewinsohn 1973). One view of depression is that the individual has lost major sources of positive reinforcement. That is, depressed individuals may lack sufficient rewards in their lives to maintain a motivation to live. When the depressed client becomes suicidal, the therapist may attempt to introduce more positive reinforcers (rewards) into his existence. To take a simple example, an elderly individual may have lost contact with friends and relatives. The absence of intimate interpersonal relationships may result in the individual's ambivalence toward living. The therapist takes the initiative in arranging for friends and relatives to visit the client regularly or help the client gain employment or find recreational outlets in a setting in which socialization plays a prominent part. Within the therapy session, the behavior therapist may also give a great deal of attention to and support for any activities related to the client's attempt to seek contacts with people.

Rational Emotive Therapy

Closely aligned with behavioral approaches is the rational-emotive therapy of Albert Ellis (1972). According to Ellis, we carry on a constant inner dialogue with ourselves. If the sentences we are saying to ourselves are rational, we will be much healthier psychologically than if we are saying irrational sentences. Maladaptive behavior is "stupid things done by unstupid people."

The person in crisis, according to this theory, may be "catastrophizing." He is devaluing himself by thinking such irrational thoughts as: "if he doesn't love me, I must be no good," or "since I lost my job, I'm worthless." The rational-emotive therapist works to help the client restructure his sentences to make them rational. From this work, which includes encouraging the client to take active measures, positive emotions are believed to follow. The emphasis for change is upon the cognitive rather than effective state.

The Crisis as a Phenomenon

The Study of Crises

The crisis concept, as well as the initial formulation of crisis theory, comes from the work of Lindemann (1944), whose interest was initially in the areas of prevention of mental disturbance and maintenance of mental health. Lindemann studied surviving friends and relatives of those killed in the tragic Cocoanut

Grove nightclub fire in Boston in 1943. He observed a specific sequence of reactions to the crisis: disorganization and tension with disruption to bodily and thought processes; preoccupation with and rumination about the past; and attempts to mobilize resources and to adjust to the situation. The crisis was then a critical point at which one could either adapt and adjust or deteriorate. Indeed, Lindmann noted that while some individuals adjusted to the loss of a friend or relative soon after the tragedy, others seemed to have abnormally long grief reactions.

Obviously, the death of a significant person in one's life is but one situation that can precipitate a crisis and set into motion either favorable or unfavorable coping behaviors. Other life changes such as divorce, marriage, birth of a child, and natural disasters frequently result in traumatic experiences. According to Caplan (1965), there are three major types of crises: developmental, individual, and institutional. *Developmental* crises include changes during certain stages of development. For example, entrance into kindergarten or the responsibilities of parenthood may bring about a crisis because the changes require a more mature level of behavior. *Individual* crises involve unexpected events such as a sudden death of a close relative. *Institutional* crises can occur when there are institutional changes such as the shift in the racial composition of a school. In general then, any of these crises can affect individuals and groups of individuals (Phillips, Martin, and Meyers 1973).

In support of Lindemann's original theory, others have found that reactions to different types of crises often adhere to predictable patterns or specific sequences (Goldenberg 1973). For example, Bowlby (1960) observed that young children went through three distinct stages after they were left in a hospital and separated from their mothers (presumably a stressful situation for children). First, the child exhibited protest behaviors in which he displayed outward distress and crying, apparently with the hope that his mother would return. Second, following protestations, there seemed to be feelings of hopelessness and despair manifested in inactivity and withdrawal behaviors. In the third stage, the child became self-absorbed, unable or perhaps unwilling to form attachments to surrounding adults.

The work of Lindemann and Bowlby helped to establish what is referred to as the "generic" approach (Jacobson, Strickler, and Morley 1968), which emphasizes the identification of characteristic behavior patterns in response to crisis (Lieb, Lipsitch, and Slaby 1973). But what accounts for differences in the way people react to stressful situations? Why do some people respond with adaptive behavior while others display maladaptive responses?

Individual Differences

According to Lindemann, the duration of bereavement reactions depends upon the success with which the person performs his "grief work." Ultimately, the grieving individual has to be emancipated from the deceased person, to readjust to the loss of the deceased in the environment, and to form new relationships. Caplan (1963) has also attempted to delineate characteristics leading to success or failure in coping with crisis. The range of favorable versus unfavorable behaviors includes the following:

1. Exploration of reality issues and direct search for information versus denial of problems with judgments based on wish fulfillment rather than reality.
2. Free expression of positive and negative feelings with high frustration tolerance versus avoidance of negative feelings.
3. Direct search for help from others versus inability to seek or accept aid from others.
4. Working through problems in manageable units versus inability to pace oneself.
5. Flexibility and ability to change versus feeling easily overwhelmed and disorganized.
6. Trust and confidence in oneself versus pessimism and distrust of one's abilities.

Support for Caplan's ideas comes from a series of studies of mothers of premature children (Caplan, Mason, and Kaplan 1965). Feeling that the mothers and their families would be under a great deal of stress, the investigators wanted to differentiate characteristics associated with favorable versus unfavorable family reactions to the premature births. Five families which were judged to have healthy outcomes exhibited a continuous concern for the situation, sought as much information about prematurity as they could, enlisted help from others, showed awareness of negative feelings, and tried to find help in dealing with the negative feelings. Five families judged to have unhealthy outcomes revealed the opposite of this pattern. Using the findings of this study, the investigators then randomly selected twenty-eight mothers and made predictions as to the quality of mother-child relations after the hospital stay. The predictions were essentially borne out. Finally, the investigators identified four major tasks that were judged essential for successful coping. Predictions of the degree to which mothers would accomplish these four tasks were made for a different group of thirty mothers of premature children. Again, the predictions were highly accurate in discriminating between favorable and unfavorable outcomes.

Other studies have examined characteristics related to successful versus unsuccessful reactions to stress. Janis reported the results of several studies dealing with stress tolerance in surgical patients (1971). He wanted to examine the relationship between the intensity of a patient's fears before surgery and his adjustment during the postoperative period. All of the patients in the study faced a highly stressful situation: they were about to undergo quite dangerous and painful operations such as the removal of a lung or part of the stomach.

Interviews and hospital observations were conducted before and after surgery. Three general patterns of emotional responses were observed in the twenty-three patients studied. The *high anticipatory fear group* of patients were constantly and deeply worried, tense, and jittery before surgery. After the operation, they had high anxiety, emotional outbursts, and excessive fears of bodily damage. The *moderate anticipatory fear group* exhibited occasional tension and worry. They sought realistic information about the operation and could engage in distracting activities. After surgery, this group was less likely to display emotional disturbance. They showed good morale and were receptive to postoperative treatment. The *low anticipatory fear group* denied feeling worried or anxious prior to surgery. They socialized, slept well, and generally felt invulnerable. Their postsurgical reaction, however, was filled with bitterness and hostility toward the hospital staff. There was acute preoccupation with their vulnerability.

As a result of these findings, Janis feels that in contrast to low or high levels of fear, a moderate amount of anticipatory fear about realistic threats is necessary if one is to develop effective coping mechanisms. Realistic and moderate fear enables a person to anticipate danger, to mentally rehearse the danger and his responses to it, to feel less helpless when the danger materializes, to have realistic expectations, and to reduce feelings of intense fear and anger.

It is clear that reactions to crises depend upon a whole host of situational factors (type of stress, number and intensity of stressors, and environmental supports and resources available) and personality factors (prior *ego* strength, experience in coping with crises, motivation to adapt, and reality orientation). If it is possible to determine those characteristics that facilitate a person's adjustment to crisis beforehand, then it is theoretically possible to prevent unfavorable reactions to crisis by helping the client to develop those appropriate characteristics. This logic may require us to go beyond crisis counseling and leads to the development of crisis prevention approaches.

Summary

Each of us has faced and will face crises in our own lives, and how we react to them may spell the difference between psychological deterioration or psychological growth. The counselor's responsibility is to facilitate the client's use of adaptive growth, producing responses during the critical juncture of a crisis.

We detailed some of the key concepts of psychoanalysis but noted that the time and money required for this treatment makes it generally inapplicable to crisis work.

We defined some general elements of crisis and discussed how individual differences play a part in response to crisis situations. As an example, we saw that a moderate degree of anxiety may prove useful in enabling people to respond to the stress of major surgery. We further delineated successful versus unsuccessful modes of responding to crisis.

Finally, we briefly examined such nonpsychoanalytic approaches as client-centered counseling, behavior modification, Gestalt therapy, and rational emotive therapy, discussing how they might be applied to the person in crisis.

References

Aguilera, D.C., J.M. Messick, and M.S. Farrell. *Crisis Intervention Theory and Methodology.* St. Louis: C.V. Mosby Co., 1970.

Alexander, F., and T.M. French. *Psychoanalytic Therapy.* New York: Ronald Press, 1946.

Bandura, A. *Principles of Behavior Modification.* New York: Holt, Rinehart and Winston, 1969.

Bowlby, J. "Separation Anxiety." *International Journal of Psychoanalysis* 41: 89-113.

Caplan, G. "Emotional Crisis." In *Encyclopedia of Mental Health* (Ed. I.A. Deutsch). Vol. 2. New York: Franklin Watts, 1963.

_____ , E.A. Mason, and D.M. Kaplan. "Four Studies in Crisis in Parents of Premature Babies." *Community Mental Health Journal* 2 (1965): 149-61.

Ellis, A. "Psychoanalysis As A Science: A Critique." *Genetic Psychology Monographs* 41: 147-212.

_____ , and R.A. Harper. *A Guide to Rational Living.* Beverly Hills, Cal.: Wilshire Books, 1961.

Erikson, E.H. *Childhood and Society.* New York: W.W. Norton, 1950.

Eysenck, H.J. "The Effects of Psychotherapy: An Evaluation." *Journal of Consulting Psychology* 16: 319-24.

Fenichel, A. *The Psychoanalytic Theory of Neurosis.* New York: W.W. Norton, 1945.

Fromm, E. *The Sane Society.* New York: Rinehart, 1955.

Goldenberg, H. *Contemporary Clinical Psychology.* Belmont, Cal.: Wadsworth, 1973.

Horney, K. *New Ways in Psychoanalysis.* New York: W.W. Norton, 1939.

Jacobson, G.J., M. Strickler, and W.E. Morley. "Generic and Individual Approaches to Crisis Intervention." *American Journal of Public Health* 58: 338-43.

_____ , D.M. Wilner, W.E. Morley, S. Schneider, M. Strickler, and G.J. Sommer. "The Scope and Practice of an Early-Access Brief Treatment Psychiatric Center." *American Journal of Psychiatry* 121: 1176-82.

Janis, I.L. *Stress and Frustration.* San Francisco: Harcourt Brace Jovanovich, 1971.

Lewinsohn, P.M. "Clinical and Theoretical Aspects of Depression." In *Innovative*

Treatment Methods in Psychotherapy (Eds. K.S. Calhoun, H.E. Adamo, and K.M. Mitchell) New York: Wiley, 1973.

Lieb, J., I.I. Lipsitch, and A.E. Slaby. *The Crisis Team: A Handbook For The Mental Health Professional.* New York: Harper & Row, 1973.

Lindemann, E. "Symptomatology and Management of Acute Grief." *American Journal of Psychiatry* 101 (1944): 101-48.

Perls, F.S., R.E. Hefferline, and P. Goodman. *Gestalt Therapy: Excitement and Growth In The Human Personality.* New York: Dell, 1965.

Phillips, B.N., R.P. Martin, and J. Meyers. "Intervention in Relation to Anxiety in School." In *Anxiety: Current Trends in Theory and Research.* (Ed. C.D. Spielberger). New York: Academic Press, 1972.

Rogers, C.R. *Client-Centered Therapy: Its Current Practice, Implications and Theory.* Boston: Houghton Mifflin, 1951.

Wolpe, J. *The Practice of Behavior Therapy.* New York: Pergamon Press, 1969.

Some Definitions of Crisis

Crisis counseling is a method of treatment designed to provide immediate help to people in a critical psychological or sociopsychological condition. A philosophy of caring is necessary to help the person in crisis, but it is not sufficient in itself; specific counseling skills and a sound conceptual background are required as well. There is a great deal of current controversy as to just what constitutes a crisis and what does not. We will present some of the dimensions of the crisis state and offer certain definitions drawn from a broadly based social science perspective. We will leave the ultimate decision of which definitions and concepts are most appropriate to the counselor, given the needs of the client.

While the word *crisis* as derived from Greek means essentially "a turning point," it would indeed be foolish to consider every turning point in one's life as a crisis. An overly broad definition could mean that practically everyone seeking counseling would be treated as if in a state of crisis; an extremely narrow definition would mean that a client under profound stress might be referred to a more casual treatment program than his situation demands. If crisis were interpreted strictly, too few persons would be served; if interpreted too liberally, crisis counseling would be employed in unwarranted cases.

Observing the frustrating attempts of theoreticians to define crisis, Schulberg and Sheldon noted: "In surveying the literature in this field, one cannot help but be struck by the arbitrary, varying and even elusive qualities currently associated with the term ... it ... remains for the most part diffident in definition, popular in usage and ambiguous in value" (1968).

Despite the inherent dangers of either a too inclusive or too exclusive definition of a crisis, we propose an outline that we hope will help keep us clear of either extreme, yet retain the strong points of both. Essential to this approach will be our emphasis on putting the needs of the client first. It is a "pragmatic" one (Lieb, Lipsitch, and Slaby 1973), and one that will emphasize a client-centered rather than a theory-centered approach (Rogers 1951).

Emergency

The terms *emergency* and *crisis* are frequently used interchangeably to designate some type of situation that needs immediate attention.

In a joint project by the American Psychiatric Association and the National Association for Mental Health, it was found that some eighty-nine definitions of

15

psychiatric emergencies were used by psychiatric hospitals and community mental health centers. Of these definitions, Frazier (1968) selected three that appear to be conceptually meaningful:

1. An emergency is any urgent psychiatric condition, functional or organic, for which immediate treatment would increase or contribute to the patient's likelihood of recovery, or provide urgently needed protection.
2. It is assumed that emergencies exist in the sphere of emotional illnesses in the same manner as they exist in the sphere of physical illness.
3. Any problem that any referring source, (minister, doctor, or other person) feels incapable of handling for even a few hours beyond the time of contracting professional help. (Published in *Psychosomatics* 9 [January-February 1968]: 7-11. Reprinted with permission.)

From these definitions it becomes clear that any attempt to find an exact definition of the term *psychiatric emergency* would lead us on an endless journey.

Definitions of Crisis

With such a diversity of opinion about the term *crisis*, it becomes a question of judgment as to which ones to present. We consider the following to be the most significant contributions so far in furthering our understanding of the crisis state. They are by no means comprehensive nor exhaustive. Rather, they are included to acquaint the crisis counselor with the scope and nature of the problem.

The *Oxford English Dictionary* defines crisis as:

The point in the progress of a disease when an important development or change takes place which is decisive of recovery or death; the turning point of a disease for better or worse.

A vitally important or decisive stage in the progress of anything, a turning point; also a state of affairs in which a decisive change for better or worse is imminent.

Williams offers a definition that has its roots in anthropology: "We may conceive of crisis . . . as a situation in which the actor faces the necessity of making an appropriate choice of action in order to avoid or minimize severe punishment" (1957). Williams limits his definition of crisis behavior to only one kind, sudden community disasters such as floods, earthquakes, and tornadoes. He expected, however, that his outline would have application to other states of crisis as well.

Hertzler adds another dimension: "No circumstance, however unusual, is a crisis unless it is so defined by human beings. The individual involved must be aware of the danger which is present or he must believe that danger is present" (1940).

To some this becomes the only way of defining a crisis (Szasz 1961). If taken alone, however, this definition overlooks the person perceived by others to be in crisis. This would include those persons who are psychotic or dangerous to themselves or others and whom friends, family members, employers, or even strangers perceive in need of help.

Maloney offers a modification of this point of view when she states that: "Crisis must be looked at through an individual's or perhaps a group's definition of it: What is a crisis to one person is an episode in zestful living to another. So, how we look at anything depends on where we stand" (1971).

Caplan's definition has been the most widely quoted. He calls it a state "provoked when a person faces an obstacle to important life goals that is, for a time, insurmountable through the utilization of customary methods of problem solving" (1961). Caplan feels that the obstacles or problems the individual is faced with in the crisis state represent a danger to him. The circumstances of the crisis situation are such that his usual ways of solving the threatening problems are not working. They are not effective enough to reduce the high level of tension and anxiety he is feeling. Crisis, according to Caplan, refers to the individual's reaction to the situation, not to the situation itself.

With such a diversity of offerings, what do most of these definitions have in common? Miller (1963) has pulled together the following common denominators:

1) The time factor
There is agreement that it is acute rather than chronic and ranges from very brief periods of time to longer periods which are not yet clearly defined. A special case is the treatment by Caplan in which the crisis situation exists from a minimum of about a week to a maximum of six to eight weeks.

2) Marked changes in behavior
The individual or group is obviously less effective than usual. Activity is related to an attempt to discharge inner tensions, there are successive trial and error abortive attempts to solve the problems without apparent success, constructive behavior decreases and frustration mounts. It is probable that a great amount of scapegoating and excuse giving occurs in this situation.

3) Subjective aspects
The person experiences feelings of helplessness and ineffectiveness in the face of what appears to be insoluble problems. There is a perception of threat or danger to important life goals of the individual and this is accompanied frequently by anxiety, fear, guilt or defensive reactions.

4) Relativistic aspects
Although there are common crisis situations, the individual's perception of threat and of a crisis is unique to him and there is some recognition that what constitutes a crisis to one individual or group does not constitute it for another group.

5) Organismic tension
The person in crisis will experience generalized physical tension which may be expressed in a variety of symptoms including those commonly associated with

anxiety. These reactions may be immediate and temporary or they may constitute a long term adjustment to the crisis situation itself. [Reproduced by permission of The Society for Applied Anthropology from *Human Organization* 22, no. 3 (Fall 1963).]

In the same year (1963) Bloom made one of the few attempts to isolate and identify some of these specific variables of the crisis state. He had eight expert judges react to a series of case histories depicting crisis situations. The five factors studied were those that he considered to have been most often identified as essential to crisis. They were: (1) knowledge or lack of knowledge of a precipitating event; (2) rapidity of onset of reaction; (3) awareness or lack of awareness of personal inner discomfort; (4) evidence of behavioral disorganization; and (5) rapidity of resolution.

To these judges, the "results of the analysis would seem to indicate that in practice, a crisis is defined primarily in terms of knowledge of a precipitating event and secondarily in terms of a slow resolution." A slow resolution was defined as occurring between one and two months.

Precipitating Events

There have been several attempts to define a crisis in terms of those precipitating events that seem to throw the client into a state of emotional distress or disorganization. Kalis, Harris, Prestwood, and Freeman established several categories of precipitating stress, all of which reflect the psychoanalytic point of view (1961). The first involves "object loss, the threat of object loss or the opportunity to restore objects." The second category, admittedly less clear, has to do with the client's contacts with previous sources of help. In this case the client has been disappointed with the help he has received, regardless of how unrealistic his or her expectations may have been. A third category has to do with the concept of identification. According to this line of reasoning, a person may become so identified with another that his or her inability to make the distinction between his own state and the other's produces crisis within him. His overidentification, then, becomes the cause of his crisis. A fourth category is labeled a "surge of unmanageable impulses." In this state, internal rather than external stimuli generate the crisis. The fifth and final category is "threat to current adjustment." This emphasizes the interaction of external events with internal conflicts. Usually the person is confronted with a situation that has both approach and avoidance characteristics, and that would require him to achieve a new homeostasis (balance) if he acted upon the new information.

Holmes and Rahe have developed what they call the "Social Readjustment Rating Scale," constituted of forty-three items that they feel are significantly related to the occurrence of disease in a person's life (1967). They define disease as a change in health status, including a broad spectrum of medical, surgical, and psychiatric disorders.

We have included their scale to serve as an indicator of significant events which crisis counselors are likely to encounter with their clients. It has been our clinical experience that these events often prove to be the key elements that must be dealt with in order for the crisis to be effectively resolved.

It is their contention that a life crisis occurs when there is a clustering of life change events within a certain period of time, sometimes within one year. They define three degrees of life crises: *mild, moderate*, and *major.* A mild life crisis occurs when there are between 150-199 LCU (life change units). A moderate life crisis occurs when there are between 200-299 LCU. A major life crisis occurs when there are over 300 LCU (Holmes and Masuda 1973). While there is some question about the validity of their predictions (Sarason 1973) the concept and the forty-three items can nevertheless prove valuable. (See Appendix A.)

In a recent study, Beck and Worthen (1972) tested the relevancy of a precipitating event in the hospitalization of persons with schizophrenic or depressive diagnoses. They conclude that

there are clear and significant differences in the life situations prior to a hospitalization of persons who are diagnosed differently. . . . As a group, schizophrenic patients are seen to decompensate in the context of life situations which are independently judged as not particularly hazardous. In contrast . . . the depressed patients were hospitalized following a clear precipitant . . . and the precipitating situation was often judged to be hazardous (Reprinted with permission from J.E. Beck and K. Worthen, "Precipitating Stress, Crisis Theory, and Hospitalization in Schizophrenia and Depression," *Archives of General Psychiatry* 26 [1972]: 128. Copyright 1972, American Medical Association.)

The question of whether or not there is a relationship between specific stress events and the occurrence of a crisis state has received attention from Eisler and Polak. They concluded that specific events such as separation, death, and losses did not invariably lead to the emergence of specific psychiatric problems (1971).

Key Elements

From this rather brief survey of the literature on precipitating factors and their relationship to crisis, what are the lessons to be kept in mind when assessing and treating someone in crisis? In the first place, it seems apparent that the presence or absence of a clearly defined precipitating event is not a safe indicator of whether or not a person is in crisis. Some persons are unable to determine just what has happened to throw them off course. Others are unwilling to share their private experience, owing either to resistance or perhaps to the feeling that they will be embarrassed or in some other way punished by their revelation. Likewise, it has been our clinical experience that a person in crisis need not be able to identify a precipitating event in order to be worked with effectively. Oftentimes clients have remarked that they don't know what happened to upset them. They simply feel overwhelmed and want some help in reducing their current state of discomfort.

Secondly, while we hold many reservations regarding the use of diagnostic labeling, the counselor may be able to formulate a more appropriate treatment plan in accordance with the presence or absence of a clear diagnostic picture. However, we caution that no single criterion such as a diagnosis be used in isolation from the overall picture in either evaluating the crisis state or determining the kind of intervention plan offered. If a person cannot identify an event or cluster of events that appear to be hazardous, obviously the counselor must not conclude that the person is either not in a crisis or psychotic.

In traditional psychoanalytic practice it is held that the precipitating event must be identified and dealt with, as it evokes some earlier unresolved conflicts. Though we do not wish to debate this point, it has been our experience that effective crisis intervention can and has taken place without the knowledge of specific precipitating events.

Thirdly, there appear to be a great many events or clusters of events that may send a person into a crisis. To spell them out completely would go far beyond the scope of this book. We have included the work of Holmes (1967) but there are others, such as Rapoport (1963), Le Masters (1957), Ichikawa (1961), all summarized in Parad (1965). However, it does make sense to conclude that as long as there are stress-producing events of any magnitude, they will have a varied impact on the coping ability of the persons facing them. If the person in crisis identifies certain events that have contributed to his present state, yet is perceived as unable to respond in an effective problem solving manner, then by his own behavioral definition, he is in a state of crisis and needs to be helped.

In view of the many definitions presented and the hazards inherent in contributing still another definition of crisis, we will say instead that while the term remains elusive, it is all too psychologically real. People who, in fantasy or reality, envision themselves to be in crisis must be attended to. Intense emotional stress deserves attention. In light of this, we feel that the counselor should be prepared to offer his or her services even if there is some question as to the degree of the client's crisis. If the counselor sees someone who turns out not to be in a "real" crisis, what harm has been done? And, hopefully, there may have been some benefit imparted to that client. From this viewpoint then, it seems that to a great extent the counselor and the client must themselves ultimately define just what constitutes a crisis and what does not, even if their definitions do not entirely coincide with those we have mentioned.

Immediacy of Service

Seeing the client quickly is part of an effective crisis service. Again quoting Kahlis et al. (1961) who emphasize at least three reasons:

(1) because circumstances associated with the disruption of functioning are more easily accessible if they are recent; (2) because only active conflicts are amenable to therapeutic intervention; (3) because disequiliberated states are more easily resolved before they have crystallized, acquired secondary gain features, or become highly maladaptive (Reprinted with permission from B. Kahlis, R. Harris, A.R. Prestwood, and L. Freeman, "Precipitating Stress As A Focus In Psychotherapy," *Archives of General Psychiatry* 5 [1961]: 225. Copyright 1961, American Medical Association.)

In practical terms this may mean that the counselor will see a client late in the evening, on a weekend, or on the same day that the request for service is made. While this is seemingly self-explanatory by virtue of the term *crisis*, the counselor will sometimes run into conflict with those who may not support this action. It is important, therefore, that the counselor educate his co-workers and supervisors concerning the need to offer services in as flexible a manner as possible. To be effective, a crisis counselor service must have as part of its foundation a philosophy of mutual support between the person delivering the service and the organization that employs him. This same principle also applies to the relationship between the community that supports the organization and the service the organization provides. Otherwise, conflicts turn into frustration and eventually into mistrust. And in these conflicts it is almost always the client who loses the most. A counselor who does not feel that he will be supported by his agency, co-workers, and community if he takes any risks, even if they are client-centered, cannot offer his best service. To enlist and maintain this support, the counselor must always be prepared to explain the actions that he took and the reasons he took them. Humanizing the delivery of a crisis service requires that the crisis counselor become committed to ongoing education for both himself and those with whom he works.

Summary

The terms *crisis* and *emergency* are often used interchangeably. Attempting to define them becomes a difficult task, and there is little consensus regarding the specific features of these concepts. Generally speaking however, the crisis state includes such features as a sudden onset of problems with marked behavior changes, accompanied by feelings of helplessness and defeat. The person perceives himself to be in a unique situation and often experiences generalized physical tension.

The presence of a precipitating event is not a requirement for effective crisis intervention to take place. Even if the client does not fulfill the criteria of the crisis state, a crisis service should be client-centered rather than theory-centered. In line with this philosophy, crisis counseling services should be made readily available to the community with the sanction and support of co-workers, administrators, and the community.

References

Beck, J.E., and K. Worthen. "Precipitating Stress, Crisis Theory, and Hospitalization in Schizophrenia and Depression." *Archives of General Psychiatry* 26 (1972): 123-29.

Bloom, B. "Definitional Aspects of the Crisis Concept." *Journal of Consulting Psychology* 27 (1963): 498-502.

Caplan, G. *An Approach to Community Mental Health.* New York: Grune & Stratton, 1961.

Eisler, R., and P. Polak. "Social Stress and Psychiatric Disorder." *Journal of Nervous and Mental Disease* 153: 227-33.

Frazier, S. "Comprehensive Management of Psychiatric Emergencies." *Psychosomatics* 9 (1968): 7-11.

Hertzler, J.O. "Crisis and Dictatorship." *American Sociological Review* V (1940): 157-69.

Holmes, T.H., and R.H. Rahe. "The Social Readjustment Rating Scale." *Journal of Psychosomatic Research* 11 (1967): 213-18.

_____, and Masuda, M. "Life Change and Illness Susceptibility." In *Symposium on Separation and Depression* (Ed. J.P. Scott and E.C. Senay). Washington, D.C.: American Association for the Advancement of Science, Publication no. 94, 1973.

Ichikawa, A. "Observations of College Students in Acute Distress (1961)." In *Crisis Intervention: Selected Readings* (Ed. Howard J. Parad). New York: Family Service Association of America, 1965.

Kahlis, B., R. Harris, A.R. Prestwood, and L. Freeman. "Precipitating Stress As A Focus In Psychotherapy." *Archives of General Psychiatry* 5 (1961): 219-26.

LeMasters, E.E. "Parenthood as Crisis." In *Crisis Intervention: Selected Readings* (Ed. Howard J. Parad). New York: Family Service Association of America, 1965.

Lieb, J., I.I. Lipsitch, and A.E. Slaby. *The Crisis Team: A Handbook For The Mental Health Professional.* New York: Harper & Row, 1973.

Maloney, E. "The Subjective And Objective Definition Of Crisis." *Perspectives in Psychiatric Care* 9 (1971): 257-68.

Miller, K. "The Concept of Crisis: Current Status And Mental Health Implications." *Human Organization* 22 (1963): 195-201.

Parad, H., ed. *Crisis Intervention: Selected Readings.* New York: Family Service Association of America, 1965.

Rapoport, Lydia. "Normal Crises, Family Structure, and Mental Health." In *Crisis Intervention: Selected Readings* (Ed. Howard J. Parad). New York: Family Service Association of America, 1965.

Rogers, C.R. *Client-Centered Therapy: Its Current Practice, Implications and Theory.* Boston: Houghton Mifflin, 1951.

Sarason, I.G., C. de Monchaux, and T. Hunt. "Methodological Issues In The Assessment Of Life Stress." In *Parameters of Emotion* (Ed. L. Levi). New York: Oxford University Press, 1973.

Schulberg, H., and A. Sheldon. "The Probability Of Crisis And Strategies For Preventive Intervention." *Archives of General Psychiatry* 18 (1968): 553-58.

Williams, H.B. "Some Functions of Communication in Crisis Behavior." *Human Organization* 16 (1957): 15-19.

Selecting the Effective Crisis Counselor

Selection of individuals to do crisis work implies identifying qualities or characteristics in persons who elicit positive therapeutic responses. In line with our emphasis upon an eclectic approach to crisis intervention, we have selected characteristics from several diverse schools of thought. It is essential to note that our eclectic approach takes into account varied points of view representative of major thinking in this field. We have carefully determined from our clinical experience and a survey of the literature that the following "non-specific" factors are essential for anyone performing any kind of counseling, though the qualities are not exclusively confined to those engaged in crisis work.

The purpose of this chapter, then, is to identify some of the factors that we feel are crucial to performing effective crisis intervention.

Emotional Maturity

One characteristic which is most frequently held forth as a valued counselor personality trait is "emotional maturity." Roche describes the emotionally mature person as having

the ability to deal constructively with reality, the capacity to adapt to change, a relative freedom from anxieties, the capacity to find more satisfaction in giving than receiving, the capacity to relate to other people in a consistent manner with mutual satisfaction and helpfulness, the capacity to sublimate, to direct one's instinctive hostile energy into creative and constructive outlets, the capacity to love (1966).

One's professional maturity may be further defined by adding the four R's of helping as defined by Carkhuff. They are: "the right of an individual to intervene in another person's life, the responsibility he must assume when he does intervene, the role he plays in the process of helping . . . and a realization of his own resources" (1969).

Communication

Communication of both verbal and nonverbal behavior is an essential skill for the counselor in crisis work. Aspects of communication which we consider essential for counselors are: (1) being able to direct or guide the therapist-client interaction to accomplish goals; (2) being able to assess if communication is taking place and to understand what is being transmitted in the interpersonal process as well as content; (3) having the ability to recognize when to speak and when to be silent; (4) being able to wait and proceed at the client's pace; and (5) being able to evaluate (Travelbee 1966).

Counselor Self-Awareness

The counselor's awareness of his own feelings is absolutely required if progress in crisis counseling is to be achieved. Because of our own life experiences, clients elicit from us strong emotions, such as anger, pity, disgust, guilt, embarrassment, and sexual feelings. It is not uncommon for the counselor to resort to self-criticism when he senses these feelings in himself. Such criticism is unwarranted unless these feelings actually interfere with the counseling process (Lieb, Lipsitch, and Slaby 1973). The more traditional way of describing this facet is embodied in the concept of counter-transference. This concept is defined as: "the attitudes and feelings, only partially conscious of the analyst . . . displaced onto the patient . . . derived from earlier situations in his own life" (Moore and Fine 1968). While there is considerable controversy among practitioners about the validity, extent, or even the basis for assuming the existence of this concept, it is our opinion that it plays a vital role in the brief counseling experience.

Empathy, Warmth, Genuineness

We consider the three therapist characteristics, described by Rogers, Truax, and Carkhuff, to be essential for anyone performing crisis work. They are: (1) empathy or understanding, (2) warmth or unconditional acceptance, and (3) unconditional positive regard or genuineness.

Empathy

The counselor who concentrates upon trying to understand the client as the client sees himself, possesses empathy (Rogers 1951). He discusses empathy in this manner:

experiencing with the client, the living of his attitudes, is not in terms of emotional identification on the counselor's part, but rather an empathic identification, where the counselor is perceiving the hates and hopes and fears of the client through immersion in an empathic process but without himself, as counselor experiencing those hates and hopes and fears.

Truax and Carkhuff define accurate empathy as involving both the therapist's ". . . sensitivity to current feelings and his verbal facility to communicate this understanding in a language attuned to the client's feelings and the meaning of those feelings. [Empathy] facilitates the patient's movement toward a deeper self-awareness and knowledge of his own feelings and experiences and their import" (1967).

Warmth

The warm, unconditional acceptance that the counselor communicates to the client enables the client to feel secure in expressing what he formerly felt was unacceptable and shameful about himself. The counselor's reflection, to the client, with complete acceptance permits the client to look at the previously unacceptable material with a certain degree of objectivity. It is this ability to view unacceptable behaviors, thoughts, and feelings with objectivity that enables the client to organize and control the unacceptable (Rogers 1951).

Rogers (1961) considers an accepting counselor as one who has warm regard for an individual as a person of "unconditional self worth." The emphasis is placed on accepting the client as a separate individual and allowing him to possess his own feelings in his own way.

Bordin defines two components of warmth (1968). The first is commitment, which is a willingness to use resources of the therapist as a substitute for those which the client lacks or which he is momentarily unable to use. The other is effort to understand, which is defined as the therapist's devotion to seeing the world as the client experiences it.

Truax and Carkhuff make the distinction between possessive and non-possessive warmth (1967). They point out that possessive warmth fosters dependence on the counselor and is conditionally given. They point out that if "the therapist himself is conditional in his warm acceptance of expressed feelings, the patient will continue to perceive 'bad feelings or thoughts' as unacceptable." They contrast this with unconditional warmth which is a "non-possessive caring for the patient as a separate person who is allowed to have his own feelings and experiences; a prizing of the patient for himself regardless of his behavior." The counselor responds to thoughts and behaviors to search out their meaning for the client rather than for approval or disapproval for himself.

Genuineness

Being genuine has been described by Rogers (1961) as being aware of one's own feelings to the extent that one's attitudes and behavior are congruent, that the counselor is as he responds, and that whatever he discloses is a real part of himself. He correlates the quality of genuineness in counselor-client relationships with the quality of helpfulness. The more genuine the counselor, the more helpful to the client this relationship becomes. According to Rogers this hypothesis holds true even when the attitudes, feelings, and thoughts conveyed would appear superficially to have a deleterious effect on the relationship. Truax and Carkhuff denote genuineness as the attitude which communicates to the client that the counselor's response is more than merely professional (1967).

The importance of genuineness in the therapeutic relationship has been approached from another point of view by Jourard (1964). He argues that self-disclosing comments by the counselor encourage similarly self-disclosing responses by the client. Furthermore, an attitude of trust develops through mutual self-disclosure. This does not mean, of course, that the counselor must reveal intimate details of his life to the client in order to be genuine, but rather, that he be willing to share with the client certain aspects of his nonprofessional existence.

Previous Functioning

It has been our observation that counselors who themselves experienced crisis with some degree of success are more apt to be able to help clients through a crisis period than those who have not. To this point Carkhuff postulates that the most useful indicator of future functioning in a counselor role is an assessment of past functioning (1969). The degree to which an individual has been able to communicate, to discriminate, and to cope successfully with past crises; his ability to be trained; and his self-awareness and insight will indicate how successful he will be as a counselor. This exploration should also include inquiry into how the counselor relates to other members of a helping profession, how he gets along with people in general, how he takes and accepts criticism, how well he deals with supervisors, and how well he learns by his mistakes.

Summary

In summary, we have identified certain personality characteristics that we consider crucial to success as a crisis counselor. In line with our emphasis upon an eclectic approach to the problems of crisis counseling, we have selected those charcteristics that we have found to be most valuable in performing the demanding work of crisis intervention.

We have not attempted to identify all of the characteristics that have been written about, only those that we have found to be particularly well suited for crisis work. We have listed such factors as emotional maturity, communication, the counselor's self-awareness, empathy, warmth, genuineness, and previous functioning as among the most significant.

References

Bordin, E.S. "The Personality of The Therapist As An Influence in Psychotherapy." *Buffalo Studies* (August 1968).

Carkhuff, R.R. *Helping and Human Relations, A Primer For Lay and Professional Helpers.* Vol. II. New York: Holt, Rinehart and Winston, 1969.

Jourard, S. *The Transparent Self.* New York: Van Nostrand, 1964.

Lieb, J., I. Lipsitch, and A. Slaby. *The Crisis Team: A Handbook For The Mental Health Professional.* New York: Harper & Row, 1973.

Moore, B.E., and B.D. Fine, eds. *A Glossary of Psychoanalytic Terms and Concepts.* Second Ed. New York: The American Psychoanalytic Association, 1968.

Roche Laboratories. *Let Your Light So Shine.* (July 1966).

Rogers, C.R. *Client-Centered Therapy.* Boston: Houghton Mifflin, 1951.

_____. *On Becoming a Person.* Boston: Houghton Mifflin, 1961.

Travelbee, J. *Interpersonal Aspects of Nursing.* Philadelphia: F.A. Davis Co., 1966.

Truax, B., and R.R. Carkhuff. *Toward Effective Counseling and Psychotherapy: Training and Practice.* Chicago: Aldine Publishing Company, 1967.

4 Goals and Techniques

The basic goal of crisis counseling is to help the person in crisis return to the level of functioning that he maintained before the crisis (Caplan 1961). It is hoped, however, that the counselor can achieve more than just that. The ideal goal is to help the client experience his crisis situation in such a way that it becomes an opportunity "to enhance the full development of the human characteristics" (Bower 1963).

Perhaps all individuals strive for a greater sense of psychological freedom and autonomy than they currently feel they possess. Feeling helpless and unable to control or understand the factors that influence one's life can have far-reaching consequences (Rotter 1966; Seligman 1974). In crisis counseling, if the counselor and client establish that expectation at the outset, there is an increased opportunity to assist the person in regaining a sense of mastery over what has happened to him. To enter into the counseling situation with the expectation of failure only adds to the burden of the crisis.

The concepts of psychological and behavioral freedom are elusive to define and must be clarified in accordance with one's frame of reference. As an example, Bower defines freedom as:

the ability of the organism to develop and maintain a resiliency and flexibility in response to a changing environment and a changing self; operationally, such freedom may be defined as the number of behavioral alternatives available in a personality under normal conditions (1963).

Kubie talks about the person's ability to learn through experience "in contrast to the freezing of behavior into patterns of unalterability" (1954). Hartman discusses "secondary autonomy," which refers to the individual's ability to adapt beyond the basic instinctual drives (1939).

It is apparent that there is no single criterion that establishes the individual's autonomous functioning and psychological freedom. Rather, a cluster of factors contribute to the life pattern of the individual and the options he has available. In line with this philosophy, Sahakian offers the following summation. Influenced by the pioneer work of Jahoda (1958), he outlines six areas:

1. the attitude of the individual toward himself, including "being aware of one's motivations; the ability to see the self realistically and correctly as opposed to an ideal self.";

2. "the successful realization of one's potentialities," which includes such concepts as self-actualization (Maslow 1968), and self-realization;
3. integration of biological, social, psychological and cultural forces, "a unifying philosophy of life, and a reasonable resistance or tolerance to stress and anxiety.";
4. "autonomy or a person's self-determination and relative independence from external influences.";
5. "the undistorted perception of reality, one free from need distortion and from loss of contact with reality"; and
6. "environmental mastery, one encompassing competency in problem-solving, adaptation or adjustment, adequate interpersonal relationships, a capacity for love, and efficiency in confronting situational requirements" (1970).

The goal of all psychotherapy then, is to help the individual achieve a greater degree of self-understanding and control. Crisis counseling may be regarded as "a kind of 'higher education' in the development of interpersonal skills and emotional capacities" (Howard and Orlinsky 1972). There is optimism in this attitude, a striving on the part of the counselor for the optimal achievement of self-actualization and fulfillment for his client. It is not to be confused with the less stringent goal of returning the client to his previous level. It is to be an addendum, a higher goal that should pervade the counseling relationship without ignoring the necessity of meeting the client where he is.

As we have noted, during a time of crisis there may be a unique opportunity for the client to secure a better understanding of how to govern his life. In our culture, crisis is so often regarded as something to be avoided that the potential for growth through crisis is too often overlooked. "Adversity," wrote Byron, "is the first path to truth."

Some of the goals in crisis counseling then, may be regarded as follows: (1) to help the person experience the crisis in such a way as to promote a greater degree of behavioral and psychological freedom; (2) to enable the client to experience a significant degree of success at mastering the crisis situation, and (3) to identify those elements that are useful in resolving the crisis state.

Techniques

In outlining some of the techniques applicable to crisis counseling, it becomes a question of choice and selection from the various schools of counseling and psychotherapy. We believe that an eclectic and broadly based social science approach is the most practical and effective way to help persons in crisis. We lean strongly toward the developing trend of the "non-school" approach (Bergin and Strupp 1972). This stance offers the counselor more latitude and flexibility in pursuing those means likely to effect a successful resolution of a crisis.

Crisis counseling always presents the counselor with unique and highly individualized situations. Even with superficially similar crisis situations, the counselor is faced with unique and unknown client problems. The nonschool approach is in line with the developing trend toward offering the techniques best suited to the client's needs, irrespective of their theoretical origin (Kiesler 1966; Strupp 1968).

In presenting the following techniques, we would like to make it clear that they are drawn from several different theoretical schools. Some techniques represent concepts that are almost exclusively identified with one particular theoretical school, such as interpretation with psychoanalysis; or assertive and relaxation training with behaviorism. There are others that cut across all schools, such as environmental manipulation. By listing them in alphabetical order we are implying that no one technique holds exclusive sway over any other. It remains for the counselor to select from among such diverse techniques, individually or in combination, that are most applicable to the immediate crisis situation.

The techniques represent more than a simple, mechanical application of words or gestures. They are instead very specialized and sensitive ways of helping individuals grow and regain some control over their lives through crisis resolution.

We are not suggesting that the following techniques are the only ones available to crisis workers. They are not! See Small (1971) for an excellent summary of some seventy-three techniques available in brief therapy. The techniques we have chosen are those that we have had some demonstrable effectiveness with given the goals of crisis intervention.

At what point does the counselor choose one technique over another? The answer to this lies with several factors: the nature and extent of the client's crisis, the degree to which the client is able to accept help, the extent of his social and community support, the personality of the counselor, and the extent of the counselor's clinical experience. In crisis work this last point can not be emphasized enough. There is no substitute for exposure to and experience with various kinds of crises, and it is this experience that the counselor must rely on in order to determine what techniques to use and when to apply them.

Assertive Training

This technique attempts to help the client counter his anxiety through the use of assertive and affirmative actions and statements. According to Wolpe:

assertive training . . . is required for patients who in interpersonal contexts have unadaptive anxiety responses that prevent them from saying or doing what is reasonable and right. . . . The therapist's interventions are aimed at augmenting every impulse toward the elicitation of these inhibited responses . . . resulting in some degree of weakening of the anxiety response habit (1969).

Wolpe cautions: "Never instigate an assertive act that is likely to have seriously punishing consequences for the patient." This can retard or stop the person from continuing to act assertively, thus strengthening the anxiety pattern the client needs to weaken. Wolpe concludes:

With a reasonable amount of . . . encouragement, most patients begin to be able to assert themselves in a matter of days, or a week or two. . . . They must be warned not to rest on their laurels, but to be alert for every opportunity for appropriate assertion. . . . The more they do, the more they can do.

In crisis counseling, the counselor will often be aware, from listening to a client's crisis, that the client's passivity in the face of overwhelming stress has added to the severity of his crisis. In such an event, the counselor may choose assertive training as one method of helping the client master his situation. In this case, the technique can be presented and discussed with the client. If the client is agreeable, then a working plan can be offered whereby the client can be assigned some homework between sessions. This homework may consist of the client keeping track of every assertive statement or action that he takes during the week. He can record this in a notebook, which can then be used as the focal point of discussion at the next counseling session. The notebook can also serve as a feedback mechanism to show the client his progress or lack of it. In conjoint work, the counselor can offer suggestions, support, and correction based upon what the client reports.

Confrontation

Essentially, confrontation means that the counselor helps the client come face to face with some of his difficulties. The counselor presents discrepancies between what the client has said and what he has done. Or the counselor may point out the difference between what is being said and the accompanying feelings. In Freudian terms, it means confronting the patient with some of his defense mechanisms, such as denial, projection, or displacement. In a sense, confrontation is a feedback procedure in which the client's behavior and apparent feelings will be presented to him in an attempt to facilitate his better understanding of what he is doing and saying. It is similar to interpretation (to be discussed later), with the exception that confrontation is a much more active and direct technique. Bellak and Small urge caution in the use of this technique (1965). They feel that one of the dangers in confrontation is that it may increase the client's use of denial and repression. Another danger is the potential eruption of a panic state, resulting in the client's fleeing from treatment. Still another problem, they warn, is the possibility of a resulting state of severe depression.

The current trend toward a more humanistic and genuine counseling approach, with its emphasis upon honesty and directness, underscores the potential danger of overutilizing confrontation. Honesty regarding one's feelings can also be used in a very hostile and punishing way. Tact and sensitivity need not be set aside, even though the counselor may feel that confrontation is in order. Gelb and Ulman state: "Immediate, active, emphatic and accurate confrontation of the patient with examples of his neurotic functioning is more effective than passive working through" (1967).

As part of the consideration of this technique, the counselor's own feelings must be taken into account. Such self-evaluative questions as "Am I angry at this client?" or "Has this situation upset me because of some unresolved conflicts that I have? Therefore, do I want to punish or withdraw from this client through confrontation?" should be asked by the counselor as part of the edict "Know thyself." The concept of countertransference also becomes an aspect of this and other techniques.

Environmental Manipulation

"Environmental Manipulation is an approach to therapy which attempts to deal with the patient's emotional disturbance by removing or modifying disorganizing elements in his environment" (Wolberg 1954). This clearly ranks as one of the more important crisis counseling measures. In crisis situations the counselor must make available to the client a variety of courses of action. Providing psychological understanding of the nature of the client's difficulties may simply not be enough. At times it will take a certain amount of maneuvering and conscious manipulation on the counselor's part to relieve some of the more serious elements of the client's crisis. Social work, for example, has long been identified with this technique. More recently, public health nurses, community psychiatrists, and community mental health workers have adopted this technique in their work. Practical help in the form of jobs, public health, housing, public assistance, and the like can often go a long way in helping someone out of an extremely difficult situation. Furthermore, it helps establish the counselor's credibility as a genuine helper. Bellak and Small (1965) favor the use of this technique in situations in which there is imminent danger to a patient's life, where job training is likely to increase self-esteem, where rehabilitation measures will increase the social functioning of formerly psychotic patients, and where volunteer work will provide appropriate outlets for persons with sexual identity difficulties. In addition, the use of social service resources such as halfway houses, art and dance therapy groups, foster homes, and free clinics can be effective in the treatment of people in crisis.

Every counselor should seek a very thorough understanding of the various community resources that he can make available to his clients. Particularly useful is knowledge regarding: the Public Assistance Department, Public Health

Department, school counseling resources, off-campus schools, alternative schools, aging services, alcoholic and mental health services, crash pads, walk-in drug and medical clinics, residential treatment centers, gay counseling resources, human potential centers, and the like. These resources will assist the counselor in the use of environmental manipulation.

Feedback

In psychotherapy, one of the basic questions asked is whether or not knowing about the correctness or incorrectness of a response, idea, or feeling improves the individual's learning. According to Watson and Tharp, the answer is a clear and resounding Yes! "The more knowledge of results a person receives about his performance, the greater is his learning" (1972). However, they add that simply providing knowledge without some kind of social reinforcement such as saying "right" may not be sufficient for learning to occur. While this is a rather murky research question, we advise that the counselor combine the two factors, feedback and social reinforcement, in using the feedback technique.

Feedback is somewhat similar to confrontation and interpretation. However, with feedback, as we intend its use, the counselor is to employ such techniques as role playing, role rehearsal, modeling, behavioral diaries, tape recorders, and the like. These approaches can be used during the session or between appointments. With time at a premium, the counselor will not want to wait unnecessarily if he can instead provide some immediate relief. Therefore, actively intervening through the use of various methods that are likely to be effective is clearly in order.

Eisler and Hersen (1973) apply this technique to their work with families in crisis:

Feedback . . . can . . . be used to give individuals information as to how their behavior affects other family members. It can also be used to show the family as a unit its difficulties in effective problem solving. . . . Additionally, feedback can be used to point out confused or inconsistent communications. . . . The purpose of initial feedback therefore is to clarify precisely what is effective and what is ineffective about the family's problem solving communication. (Reprinted with permission from R. Eisler and M. Herson, "Behavior Techniques In Family-Oriented Crisis Intervention," *Archives of General Psychiatry* 28 [1973]: 112. Copyright 1973, American Medical Association.)

Interpretation

In this type of intervention the chief goal is to achieve change by adding to the client's awareness of his behavior and psychological processes. Interpretation can be based on the here and now, or it can be based on past events. It is a specialized way of helping the client achieve an understanding of cause-and-effect relationships in his life. Interpretation is the mainstay of insight therapy and has long been used by Freudian analysts. Although until recently it has been reserved for long-term counseling situations, Bellak and Small maintain that it is also a useful technique in brief counseling situations if used thoughtfully (1965).

Insight is thought to facilitate change, and interpretation is directed toward the achievement of insight. Briefly, it has been suggested that interpretation can be used to deal with dependency (Malan 1963), reality (Gould 1966), psychological defenses (Lewin 1965), symptom meanings (Saul 1951), precipitating events (Harris, et al. 1963), and acute depression (Coleman 1960).

There is, however, considerable disagreement as to the extent and depth of interpretation which is most effective. Wolk urges that interpretation should be geared to leave a client with a minimal amount of anxiety at the end of an interview (1967). This is a sound idea and one with which we strongly agree. The counselor should avoid at almost all costs introducing seriously disturbing material with someone who is in severe crisis, and we feel that such material should never be introduced near the end of the session.

It is also useful to avoid being dogmatic in making interpretations. For example, "It seems to me that your leaving your wife might reflect a general dissatisfaction with your life" is far superior to "It's obvious that you're leaving your wife for things which are your own fault."

It is also unwise to force your interpretation on a client when he does not accept it. It is one thing to overcome a client's minor resistance to your interpretation of his motives or behavior, quite another to insist that you are right even if he adamantly refuses to believe you. Ultimately, interpretation, no matter how valid, is useful only to the extent that the client is able to accept and use it.

Modeling

Modeling is a technique in which the behavior of others who have successfully achieved a desired goal is used as a model for the client who has not yet achieved that goal (Watson and Thorp 1972). By selectively choosing a model who achieves the goals that the client wishes to attain, the client can observe the exact sequence of behaviors likely to lead to his own successful mastery of the problem.

There are elements of modeling in all interpersonal transactions. And as a matter of fact, modeling—or learning by imitation—is commonly the primary way in which intricate and complicated social behaviors are learned during childhood. In a crisis situation, the counselor may want to make use of modeling by urging the client to observe or talk with someone who has successfully mastered some of the problem areas that he is having difficulty with, or by having the client model the counselor in some simulated role-playing situation.

Modeling can be used in conjunction with several other techniques, such as assertive and relaxation training. It may also be used to facilitate the client's self-disclosures in those instances in which the client feels extremely inhibited.

Reassurance

Reassurance is likely to play a part in all forms of counseling and psychotherapy (Wolberg 1954). It is the act of trying to free someone from fear and anxiety and restoring their self-confidence. It is, according to Garner "a special type of activity directed . . . at alleviating the patient's anxiety; giving moral support to a viewpoint or action; suggesting and directing channels of activity, behavior, and attitudes which correct a fault, diminish need for guilt feelings and encourage constructive, realistic achievement" (1970).

In crisis work, reassurance can be a positive and particularly helpful technique. This is especially the case when the client is anxious about his ability to pull himself out of his crisis, or when he is unable to see much hope for relief in the future. Frequently, clients will ask if what they are going through is a forerunner to a nervous breakdown. "Am I going crazy?" and "I must be losing my mind" are frequent thoughts, if not overtly expressed fears.

When clients are experiencing these apprehensions, it can be quite helpful if the counselor will offer reassurance to the effect that the client's fears are unrealistic. This, in part, can be accomplished by "normalizing" the crisis experience. That is, the counselor can point out the normal features of the crisis state (see Chapter 2), and that crisis is a part of living. When the counselor is able to support this with some specific data, it may have some more effective impact (Bellack and Small 1966). Where the client is more or less convinced by the counselor's authority, knowledge, and sincerity that the counselor can be trusted, reassurance can become a powerful technique. Caution should be exercised however, and reassurance should not be offered at the drop of a hat. For example, it would be unwise to give the impression that a severe, lifelong personality disturbance is "only normal," or that it will disappear without professional counseling. This would falsely raise the client's hopes and result in later disappointment. Counseling experience, good supervision, and client feed-back will assist in the task of knowing how and when to use reassurance.

Relaxation Training

Physical relaxation as a means of dealing effectively with anxiety has been advised by therapists of various theoretical backgrounds (Ferenczi 1951; Jacobson 1934; Wolpe 1969).

Specifically, this technique requires that the counselor instruct the client in progressive muscular relaxation. This training may even be initiated in the first interview if therapeutically appropriate. The following method has been found quite useful in promoting relaxation and reducing anxiety and tension.

The counselor asks the client to sit in a comfortable chair, feet firmly planted on the floor, arms either resting in his lap or on the arms of the chair, and his head leaning back against the wall, eyes closed.

Next the client is asked to visualize what his muscles look like throughout his body. He is asked to imagine the muscles in his arms, legs, neck, back, and so forth. Those persons who have a hard time doing this can be assisted by having the counselor show them pictures or diagrams of the muscular system.

Next the client is asked to tighten briefly a group of muscles, say those of the right hand and arm. Then he is to relax and begin to visualize what his muscles look like while he concentrates on their becoming relaxed. During this time the counselor is verbally instructing the client. He may say, slowly, "I want you to concentrate on relaxing those muscles in the hand. Imagine what they look like while they are getting soft and relaxed. First the muscles on the right side—then on the other side of the hand—relaxing all the time, concentrating upon loosening those muscles and relaxing."

This procedure is then followed throughout the whole body, section by section. Allow approximately twenty minutes per session and divide the body into roughly five groups: head and neck, arms and hands, upper part of the body, lower part of the trunk, and legs and feet.

Between sessions have the client practice approximately fifteen to twenty minutes a day. This will enable him to master the technique much more rapidly.

The speed with which the client masters this technique will influence the method by which the counselor will administer it and how fast he will proceed from session to session. We also advise the use of Jacobson's book as a way for the client to improve his relaxation skills. It is available at many local bookstores.

There have been a great many relaxation techniques developed in recent years. One of them, the Schade technique, involves a systematic lengthening of the exhalation phase of breathing, paired with suggestions of muscular relaxation. It is quite possible that an "alpha state" may be attained with this technique. It is also particularly useful in Wolpe-type desensitization work. This technique differs from the Jacobson method in that it does not involve the preliminary tensing of muscles. This is thought by some to be an advantage.

Self-Disclosure

Self-disclosure by the counselor may have a positive impact on the client, and the degree to which the counselor is willing to disclose something about himself may be a factor in the subsequent willingness of the client to reveal deeply personal information (Jourard and Jaffe 1970). This has been a contention of many Gestaltists all along and one factor they consider to be an essential element in the healing process of crisis work (Fagan and Shepherd 1970). It has been our experience however, that persons in crisis are generally under a considerable amount of pressure to begin with and need very little prompting to get them to talk about themselves and their conflicts. As a general rule, we feel that the crisis counselor should serve more as a model of facilitation rather than as a self-discloser. However, in those instances in which the counselor finds clients unable to discuss certain matters, disclosing personal material about himself may be considered an appropriate technique. It is a form of modeling. But keep in mind that the client is not there to help work out the counselor's conflicts. The counselor has such resources as his supervisor, professional peers, and psychotherapy, while the client must rely chiefly upon the counselor.

Ventilation

"This is a metaphor describing the act of freely expressing one's emotions, feelings and thoughts, particularly about a problem" (Small 1971). It is the act of letting the client "get things off his chest" in an atmosphere of relative safety and acceptance.

Wolberg says:

Ventilation by the person of his fears, hopes, ambitions, and demands often gives him relief, particularly when his verbalizations are subjected to the uncritical and sympathetic appraisal of the listener. . . . The ability to share his secrets . . . robs the [negative] experiences of much of their frightening quality. In addition the patient finds his judgment . . . of his experiences may have been distorted (1954).

Ventilation requires that the counselor pay careful attention to what the client is saying and feeling about himself and his crisis. Ivey uses the term "attending behavior." He defines this as simply listening, and he then offers some specifics about how to achieve this behavior:

The counselor should *look at* his client to note postural movements, gestures, and facial expressions . . . it should be natural looking. . . . Secondly . . . the interviewer is relaxed. . . . Finally, *verbal following* behavior demands that the counselor respond to the last comment or some preceding comment . . . without introducing new data . . . [no] topic jumping or asking questions in a random pattern (1971).

Ventilation as a technique has been used in a variety of settings and in a variety of counseling situations. Keller (1960) and Cook (1966) have used it in individual and group therapy with hospitalized patients; Hanson recommends it in the treatment of medical emergencies (1966); Lindemann finds this to be one of the most effective techniques in his work with acute grief (1944); Kubler-Ross likewise expounds its use in work with the dying (1969); Rothenberg encourages its use with children who need brief counseling (1955).

Suicidal/Homicidal Assessment

Whenever the counselor sees a client who is displaying potentially suicidal types of behaviors, thoughts, or feelings, he must pay careful attention to those messages. It is essential to listen to every suicidal message thoughtfully. It is unwise to assume anything until there is evidence to support the seriousness of the material, or the lack of it. Ask specific questions! The client is not going to be frightened because he's asked about his suicidal impulses and thoughts. The counselor will not be giving him ideas. On the contrary, if the questions *are not* asked, the implication given is that the counselor is so uneasy about this subject matter that he wishes to avoid it. Hence, the client is to avoid it as well since it is apparently so unpleasant. The counselor will want to be familiar with the suicidal assessment material in Appendix B.

There is no single item that determines the seriousness of a client's suicidal potential. Rather, it is a cluster of events taken together that lends some significant clue to the suicidal potential. The questions of *Who*: who was around at the time of the gesture? who might the suicidal message be aimed at? *What*: what was the method? what were the circumstances surrounding the attempt? what might have been the aim? was it for attention, manipulation? *When*: when did it occur? the time. *Where*: where did it occur and where were significant others? *Why now*: why today rather than yesterday? These questions can often be used to assist in determining the seriousness of the client's actions.

Essentially the same principles apply when evaluating a potentially homicidal person as a suicidal. (Suicide is self-murder, homicide is other-murder.) There are, of course, statistical differences in the composition of these two groups. Nevertheless, as in suicidal determination, the assessment of homicidal potential is based upon a cluster of factors rather than just one criterion.

When the counselor, based on his expertise and good judgment, comes to believe genuinely that his client is committed to a serious act of physical violence against another person, it is his ethical responsibility to make every effort to warn the potential victim of this danger. Needless to say, this determination, as with suicidal situations, often calls for consultation with skilled colleagues. The counselor should never hesitate to share his knowledge about these types of cases with his supervisor, consulting psychiatrist, and the person who has legal responsibility for the clinical performance of the worker.

Stay out of the position of being bound by the client to keep this information quiet. Confidentiality with calculated destruction to others is rarely, if ever, justified. The mere fact that the client is telling the counselor about this is sufficient indication that he wants someone to know what he is planning and thinking. This may be his only method of asking for assistance, and the counselor should therefore take the appropriate action and respond to this "cry for help."

Medication

While tranquilizing medication is not strictly a treatment technique as we have defined it so far, it nevertheless falls within the area of an important treatment method. Anyone who has worked with clients in crisis will recognize the important role psychopharmacology plays. While we do not expect every crisis counselor to become an expert in this field, we do expect the effective counselor to have some familiarity with it.

For example, it is essential to be knowledgeable regarding the various kinds of psychotropic drugs. Valzelli (1973) makes the following distinctions: (1) sedatives, (2) major tranquilizers, (3) minor tranquilizers, (4) antidepressants, and (5) psychostimulants. Among the more commonly used sedatives are, by brand name, Nembutal, Seconal, Amytal, and Penobarbital. The more commonly used major tranquilizers are Thorazine, Stelazine, and Mellaril. Miltown, Valium, Librium, and Tranxene are among the more commonly used minor tranquilizers. The most frequently prescribed antidepressants are Parnate, Marplan, Niamid, Tofranil, and Elavil. The most commonly used psychostimulants are Dexadrine, Dexamyl, and Ritalin.

In addition to this knowledge the counselor should become familiar with such psychopharmacology references as the *Physician's Desk Reference* (1974). This book will tell the counselor such basic facts as side effects, proper dosage, milligram size, color, shape, and the contraindications of the particular medication. These simple facts can prove quite useful, particularly if the counselor needs them in a hurry and the client only vaguely recalls them. On more than one occasion a counselor has reported how helpful this information was in determining the state of a client's previous psychologic history.

Furthermore, such knowledge can sometimes be helpful in determining the more precise nature of the client's crisis. By careful exploration of the client's medication history, the counselor may be able to determine something about his previous coping ability. For example, the client might present a detailed description of having been on Thorazine, and in further analysis the counselor learns that the dosage was 300 mgm three times a day. This would suggest to the counselor that the previous crisis state may have been rather severe. This information, then, might prove quite beneficial in determining the role of medication in the current crisis.

It has been our experience that on numerous occasions a counselor will come into contact with clients recently released from a psychiatric facility who are in some state of crisis. Their crisis may actually involve the fact that they have stopped taking their medications, and are falling again into an earlier, strongly maladaptive state. While their crisis might be temporarily abated through supportive counseling, they essentially need to get back on their medication. The counselor who has some working knowledge of psychopharmacological agents will be in a better position to ameliorate such a crisis through appropriate psychiatric referral and consultation.

A word of caution: the counselor should never place himself in the position of suggesting what kind of medication the client should be taking. Always leave this up to the person who is qualified. Otherwise the counselor may find himself in an awkward position with both the prescribing physician and the client.

There is little doubt that tranquilizing medication can become an important indicator in helping the perceptive counselor determine the nature and extent of a client's crisis. However, a counselor must not allow a mere history of medication to bias his opinion of the client's present psychological state.

Summary

There are two fundamental goals in crisis counseling: to enable the person in crisis to regain the capacity to deal effectively with the crisis and to regain his equilibrium; and to enable him to grow from the crisis experience, to increase his mastery over his own behavior and gain greater self-awareness.

In this chapter we discussed several techniques the counselor should find useful in attaining these goals. An awareness of these, among others, will increase the options available to the counselor, thus increasing his probability of success.

References

Bellak, L., and L. Small. *Emergency Psychotherapy and Brief Psychotherapy.* New York: Grune & Stratton, 1965.

Bergin, A.E., and H.H. Strupp. *Changing Frontiers in The Science of Psychotherapy.* Chicago: Aldine-Atherton, 1972.

Bower, E.M. "Primary Prevention of Mental and Emotional Disorders: A Conceptual Framework and Action Possibilities." *American Journal of Orthopsychiatry* 33 (1963): 832-48.

Caplan, G. *An Approach to Community Mental Health.* New York: Grune & Stratton, 1961.

Coleman, M.D. "Methods of Psychotherapy: Emergency Psychotherapy." In *Progress in Psychotherapy* (Eds. J.H. Wasserman and J.L. Moreno). Vol. 5. New York: Grune & Stratton, 1960.

Cook, E.L. "Short-Term Group Therapy." *Journal of Medical Sociology* 63 (1966): 83.

Eisler, R., and M. Herson. "Behavior Techniques In Family-Oriented Crisis Intervention." *Archives of General Psychiatry* 28 (1973): 111-16.

Fagan, J., and I.L. Shepherd, eds. *Gestalt Therapy Now.* New York: Harper and Row, 1970.

Ferenczi, S. "Contra-Indications To The Active Psychoanalytic Technique." *Further Contributions To The Theory and Techniques of Psychoanalysis.* New York: Basic Books, 1951.

Garner, H.H. "Psychotherapy And Confrontation Technique Theory." *Psychotherapy.* St. Louis: Warren Green, Inc., 1970.

Gelb, L.A., and M. Ulman. "Instant Psychotherapy Offered At An Out-Patient Psychiatric Clinic." *Frontiers of Hospital Psychiatry* 4:14 (August 1967).

Gould, R.I. "Emergencies In The Out-Patient Department." In *Emergency Psychiatry and Brief Therapy.* (Eds. G.J. Wayne and R.R. Koegler.) Boston: Little, Brown, 1966.

Hanson, D.D. "Psychological Aspects of Medical Emergencies: An Internist's View." In *Emergency Psychiatry and Brief Therapy.* (Eds. G.J. Wayne and R.R. Koegler.) Boston: Little, Brown, 1966.

Harris, M.R., B.L. Kalis, and E.H. Freeman. "Precipitating Stress: An Approach To Brief Therapy." *American Journal Psychotherapy* 17 (1963): 465-71.

Hartmann, H. *Ego Psychology and The Problem of Adaptation.* New York: International University Press, 1939.

Howard, K.I., and D.E. Orlinsky. "Psychotherapeutic Processes." *Annual Review of Psychology.* Vol. 23. Palo Alto, Cal.: Annual Review, Inc., 1972.

Ivey, A.E. *Microcounseling: Innovations in Interviewing Training.* Springfield, Ill.: Charles C. Thomas, 1971.

Jacobson, E. *You Must Relax.* Chicago: University of Chicago Press, 1934.

Jahoda, M. *Current Concepts of Positive Mental Health.* New York: Basic Books, 1958.

Jourard, S., and P. Jaffe. "Influence Of An Interviewer's Disclosure On The Self-Disclosing Behavior of Interviewees." *Journal of Counseling Psychology* 17 (1970): 252-57.

Keller, M.H. "Short Term Group Therapy With Hospitalized Non-Psychotic Patients." *North Carolina Medical Journal* 21 (1960): 228-31.

Kiesler, D.J. "Some Myths Of Psychotherapy Research And The Search For A Paradigm." *Psychological Bulletin* 65 (1966): 110-36.

Kubie, L.S. "The Fundamental Nature Of The Distinction Between Normality and Neurosis." *Psychoanalytic Quarterly* 23 (1954): 183.

Kubler-Ross, E. *On Death & Dying.* New York: The Macmillan Company, 1969.

Lewin, K.K. "A Brief Psychotherapy Method." *Pennsylvania Medical Journal* 68 (1965).

Lindemann, E. "Symptomatology and Management of Acute Grief." *American Journal of Psychiatry* 101 (1944): 101-48.

Malan, D.H. *A Study of Brief Psychotherapy*. London: Tavistock Publications, 1963.

Maslow, A.H. *Toward a Psychology of Being*. Princeton, N.J.: Van Nostrand, 1968.

Physician's Desk Reference, 1974. 28th Ed. Oradell, N.J.: Medical Economics.

Rothenberg, S. "Brief Psycho-Dynamically Oriented Therapy." *Psychosomatic Medicine* 17 (1955): 455-57.

Rotter, J.B. "Generalized Expectancies for Internal Versus External Control of Reinforcement." *Psychological Monographs: General & Applied* 80 (1966): 1-28.

Sahakian, W.S. *Psychopathology Today*. Itasca, Ill.: F.E. Peacock Publishers, Inc., 1970.

Saul, L.J. "On The Value of One Or Two Interviews." *Psychoanalytic Quarterly* 20 (1951): 613-15.

Seligman, M. "Depression and Learned Helplessness." In *The Psychology of Depression: Contemporary Theory and Research* (Eds. R.J. Freedman and M.M. Katz). Washington, D.C.: V.H. Winston (in press).

Small, L. *The Briefer Psychotherapies*. New York: Brunner/Mazel, 1971.

Strupp, H.H. "Overview and Developments In Psychoanalytic Therapy: Individual Treatment." *Modern Psychoanalysis and Perspectives*. (Ed. J. Mormor.) New York: Basic Books, 1968.

Valzelli, L. *Psychopharmacology: An Introduction to Experimental and Clinical Principles*. Flushing, N.Y.: Spectrum Publications, 1973.

Watson, D.L., and R.G. Thorp. *Self-Directed Behavior: Self Modification For Personal Adjustment*. Monterey, Cal.: Brooks/Cole Publishing Company, 1972.

Wolberg, L.R. *The Technique of Psychotherapy*. New York: Grune and Stratton, 1954.

Wolk, R.L. "The Kernel Interview." In *Journal Long Island Consult. Center* 5:1 (1967).

Wolpe, J. *The Practice of Behavior Therapy*. New York: Pergamon, 1969.

Interviewing in Crisis Intervention: The Beginning

Crisis counselors report that they frequently feel a certain amount of anxiety and excitement just prior to their initial meeting with a client, no matter how many times they have gone through the experience before. This certainly makes sense when one considers how many tasks the counselor must be prepared to deal with in that first interview.

This chapter outlines some of the key elements of the beginning phase so as to increase the counselor's sense of mastery of the interview. Another goal is to help him function more effectively as the designated crisis intervenor.

Beginning Preparation

The beginning phase actually gets uder way before the counselor ever sees the client. It begins when the counselor first starts to get information about the person in crisis. In an agency, this may occur when the receptionist or intake worker says: "You have a woman coming to see you who is very upset and crying" or "This husband is on the phone saying he is depressed and upset because his wife has just left him and he wants to kill himself."

While the actual face-to-face interview or telephone contact may be several minutes away, the alert counselor is already beginning to formulate in his mind some general ideas about what he is going to do and what the nature of the crisis might be. The counselor begins to go over the kinds of things that he will want to accomplish with the case, keeping in mind such questions as:

1. Why is the client seeking help now?
2. What is the client's current level of functioning?
3. What are the goals of this interview?
4. What are the techniques to be used to accomplish these goals?
5. What resources can be used to help this client?

Our experience has shown us that by going through a specific checklist prior to beginning the interview, the counselor is less anxious and more alert to handle the demands that will be placed on him. This can be particularly helpful to the counselor who is seeing a client for the first time, and who wants to do a good job but is nervous about all that he has to remember.

In addition to this mental rehearsal, relaxation techniques can be very helpful. Wolpe (1969), and Jacobson (1934) before him, suggested some very specific muscle-relaxation techniques that were effective in countering fear and anxiety. This approach has been used extensively with people who have been unusually afraid of such things as high places, snakes, public speaking, etc. The procedure is fairly simple and easily learned and has been dealt with in Chapter 4.

Preparation also means that the counselor must temporarily suspend his thinking about the client with whom he has been previously involved. Often in crisis counseling—particularly if it is practiced in a drop-in clinic or with a crisis service—there may be several persons scheduled to speak with a counselor, sometimes one right after another. The counselor who is still involved in thinking about the previous crisis will not be alert to all the facets of the new situation, thereby cutting into his effectiveness with the new case.

It is therefore appropriate for the counselor to say to himself and others that he needs a few minutes to himself before beginning the next interview. As clear as this principle may appear to be, it is quite easy to forget, particularly when there are pressures from the client's family members and his friends to do something immediately. The counselor must not allow himself to be pushed into seeing a new client until he feels he has gotten the last case pretty well taken care of and is prepared for the next. Of course, there are exceptions, such as potential life-and-death situations, but as a rule the counselor should try to set some limits on the demands made upon him to act before he has himself grasped the situation. In the long run both the clients and the counselor will benefit.

In accordance with the circumstances of the crisis situation, the counselor should try at the outset to make clear the purpose of the interview and to whom the client is speaking. We emphasize here that this introduction should depend on the nature of the crisis, the state of mind the client is in, the setting of the interview, and so forth. It has been our experience that when first meeting a client the counselor's introduction must be one that does not immediately commit the counselor to a narrow response but is flexible and subject to adaptation depending on his client's reaction. Some examples of appropriate and inappropriate introductions will help make this point clearer:

Appropriate

Counselor: My name is Kay C. I'm the crisis counselor. Can you—

Client: Right now I'm very worried about myself. I mean being able to live without my husband (long pause, starts to cry) and just the low feelings I have about myself. I can forget about it, but I always have to come back to the house and go to bed alone at night . . . .

Counselor: I'm Carol M., a crisis counselor. Would you like to just—

Client: I am divorced. My husband and I have recently remarried, but tonight I have the feeling he doesn't want me there. In fact he is sitting in the car right now . . . .

Counselor: My name is Mr. Alberstein. I'm the crisis counselor on today. I'm here to help people who are in crisis and will work with you through your crisis. Now, could you tell me about yourself?

Client: My wife has taken an overdose of tranquilizers many times in the last two years. She took an overdose with a bottle of booze. It wouldn't make any difference if she had a drink or a lot of drinks, the reaction would be the same . . . .

For contrast, we include several examples of inappropriate introductions.

Inappropriate

Counselor: You said you talked to Mary Ann and what made me think of asking this is you felt like maybe it was ten or fifteen minutes where you—

Client: It was ten minutes.

Counselor: I have to establish one thing in our first interview and that is the fee. It says here that you are on social security or is that your—

Client: No, my father is receiving it. I am not willing to pay anyone associated with this place. I do not feel that I need to be here.

Counselor: Okay. Let's get back to the fee. How about out of the seventy-five dollars, a five-dollar fee?

Client: No.

A client in crisis is seeking immediate help and support. His severe anxiety will not be alleviated unless he is given good reason to feel that he is understood by, and in turn understands, the crisis counselor. For this reason it is essential that the counselor use terms that are comprehensible to the client and avoid terms that only serve to create additional anxiety and misunderstanding.

In the three appropriate examples the introductions were clear, concise, and flexible enough to meet the client at his immediate level of functioning. By contrast, the last two introductions were confusing and quite inappropriate for the crisis situation.

Goals of Interviewing

Gathering Information

Broadly speaking, the goal of every initial crisis interview is to gather, collect, and organize information about the client's crisis (Sullivan 1954). This means that the counselor will have to be as alert as possible while listening to and observing his client. Some of the things to look for are outlined below. However, the counselor should always keep in mind that this is not all there is to it. Keeping track of bits and pieces of information that are only heard once or twice during the course of the interview requires a great deal of practice, and even then important themes are sometimes overlooked, forgotten, or missed altogether. In addition, the counselor wants to remember to ask questions about things that are unclear or contradictory. To do this the counselor is required to develop his short-term memory capacity. These and other factors, such as keeping track of the time, tying together related informational themes, and enabling the client to talk about his crisis, all influence the reporting, collecting, and recalling of information.

Informational themes are those ideas or sets of facts that appear to be dominant or persistent throughout the course of the interview. Identifying these themes constitutes one of the more important tasks for the counselor if he is to grasp a comprehensive picture of his client's crisis. These themes are identified as the first step in the deductive model discussed later in this chapter.

The following are some of the questions that should be answered in the first interview whenever possible:

1. What prompted the client to seek help now?
2. What happened that caused this crisis?
3. How is the client trying to solve the crisis? What is working? What is not working?
4. How was the client behaving before the crisis?
5. How is he behaving now?
6. Has anything like this happened before? How was it handled?
7. What is the client's history of handling other crises? What was successful? What was not successful?
8. What are the client's psychological strengths?
9. What are the client's environmental (family, leisure, work, religion, etc.) strengths?
10. What does the client see as the two or three most important problems to be worked on immediately?
11. How much immediate success is he likely to have in these or other problem areas?
12. How life-threatening is this situation? Immediately? In the near future?
13. What things are likely to stand in the way of successful crisis resolution?
14. What is the client's mental status?

Having these questions in mind, the counselor needs some outline within which to fit the interview material. The deductive model appears to be effective for this purpose.

Deductive Model

During a crisis interview a client will frequently give the counselor a great deal of information about himself and his crisis. Oftentimes this information will come pouring out in such rapid fashion that if the counselor is not prepared, he can get confused and overwhelmed, missing valuable points. Since all of this information is so important to the counselor in forming a comprehensive picture of his client's crisis, it is necessary to have some kind of plan regarding the organization of this information. The deductive model is an example of such an organizational plan.

The deductive model provides the counselor with a way of identifying and organizing client information that will facilitate the process of crisis resolution. We stated earlier that the goal of each interview was to get information about such things as precipitating events, strengths, deficits, previous coping experience, and so forth. With this as the goal, then, some diagram of how to catalog all this data is necessary.

This model permits the counselor to keep track of things in a systematic and logical way, first by keeping a list of the things the client says and then by filtering out the relevant from the irrelevant information, moving from left to right on the chart.

This model emphasizes the importance of the early part of the initial interview. It has often been our experience that within the first ten to twenty minutes of the interview, many of the important facts of the client's crisis will emerge. If the counselor will keep this in mind, then he will begin immediately keeping track of what the client tells him, even during the first ten to twenty seconds. With practice and experience, the counselor can increase his skills at early formulation of informational themes and a crisis resolution plan.

This model is not intended to exclude other designs for gathering and organizing facts, nor is it intended to imply that the crisis information will always fall into these neat categories. It does, however, offer a plan or a mental map that will assist the counselor in keeping track of things in a way that may reduce confusion. With practice and rehearsal, along with some other teaching aids like a tape recorder or an observer, this technique can be mastered to the benefit of both client and counselor.

The following is the first five minutes of a tape-recorded interview that is fairly typical of many crisis situations. It is presented almost entirely intact for the purpose of demonstrating how a counselor might use the deductive model in actual practice.

Many of the major crisis themes have been isolated in actual practice by a variety of counselors in training, most of whom report that after a few concentrated attempts they are able to employ the model successfully. These counselors have found the method helpful during the initial phase of the interview.

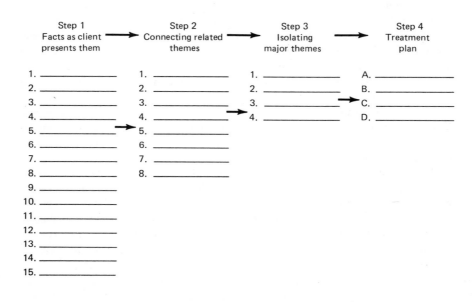

Figure 5-1. A Deductive Model for Crisis Counseling

Mrs. H., thirty: Everything has happened all at once to me and I've got to the point I just can't cope. I cry easy. If I cry it's just me. I can't help it, I cry. I've become manic depressive. I've always been one to let things bother me. I've always been really, really, insecure. Everything was going fine and about a month ago my husband developed a blood clot in his leg and he was put in the hospital. Well, this upset me. It shouldn't have, but it did. I went to pieces. I have a little boy, seven, that is retarded and a little girl that's normal, and I have no family or anyone here to help me with the kids and baby sitting, so at night, to visit my husband, I was sending the kids off to friends.

I'm very dependent upon my husband. Very. When he was put in the hospital I guess this just did it. He was gone, I was on my own, and I had to function. Well, I couldn't fix meals, I just couldn't do anything. So even though the doctor said don't worry, I didn't believe it. I kept thinking it was worse. He was in the hospital a week and the clot dissolved. He was on Coumadin [a commonly used drug to dissolve blood clots] when he came home. When he came home he was very tired. This wasn't like my husband. He's not the kind to lay down on the couch at eight-thirty and fall asleep. He's one that will get up at ten o'clock at night and bake cookies. I realize all of us who have been laid up in a hospital for a week are bound to be a little tired. I knew it wasn't like my husband, so this upset me. I didn't believe the doctor. I didn't feel he was taking good enough care. He was on this Coumadin, and he started to bruise easily, and then his ankles swoll up and I couldn't accept that. I thought if he's home from the hospital and the clot has dissolved, he should be getting better.

Then two weeks ago this coming Friday I was fired. I had been with them part time because we just recently, last year, bought a house. I just work for the house payment. I don't work for spending money or anything like that. I just do it to pay the house payment. I was fired unfairly. There was no reason for me to be fired. I worked for this bank, and there was an older man there who was fifty years old. He was a manager, but he is very childish and very crotchety and one of these that wasn't specific. He would bring me things and he wouldn't explain what to do, and I'm not a mind reader. I didn't know what he wanted. I had only been there four months. So we had a communication problem, but being a sensitive person I didn't pick it up. I didn't feel that there was a communication problem. I just didn't make that big a deal of it. And my boss kept saying, "Sue, is there a communication problem between you and Frank?" and I kept saying no. It was a shock to me. And he said, "Frank claims he can't communicate with you." So he talked to me again one time, and then Thursday he said, "I hate to tell you this, but we've given you two-weeks notice."

Well, what a time to have this happen. You know, my husband not getting better as far as I can see, and I lose my job. I can't find one. I feel there are so many women, now that their kids are in school, looking for work just for spending money, and I need a job because we'll lose our house.

Then Saturday night, well since last Tuesday, my husband complained of stomach cramps. I have had them too just from nerves, but I know he's not nervous. So Saturday night about midnight he said, "Those pains are getting worse," and I said, "Call the doctor." So he did, and he said to the doctor, "I passed blood." Well, he didn't tell me this and immediately I blew it out of proportion and had him bleeding internally. The doctor said to stop the Coumadin and so Joe went in Monday. He said, "It's the body's way of saying I've had enough of this blood thinning, and you need to stop."

Monday afternoon I called Dr. B. and said, "Look, I'm very upset about this." He's walking around with blood inside of him and my mother died of internal bleeding. He's not a doctor to really go into detail and explain and say, "Look, everything is okay." He just doesn't tell me about anything. So he talked to me and said maybe I was worrying about nothing, and that I was blowing things out of proportion, and I started to cry. Then he realized I really am upset about this whole business and . . . plus having a retarded boy. He's not badly retarded. He doesn't look retarded. He has the kind where they are heavy. He can't get rid of the sugar in his system, so he's fat and he's a compulsive eater. Normally I wouldn't hit him for sneaking food, but I have just been hitting and beating on him and things like that. If something more happens to me, I won't be able to take it. I've just had it. (*Begins to cry*.) [See facing page for deductive model.]

As this chapter is devoted to the beginning of the crisis interview, we will focus here only on step 1 of the model. In subsequent chapters we will examine the other steps. The following case example, then, demonstrates the application of step 1 to the first ten minutes of the interview.

Mrs. S., thirty-five: Well, first of all I always start crying. (*Beginning to cry*.) I don't really know what my problem is. I just get upset all the time. I started to go through the change some time ago. I take medication for that. My kids left home and I quit smoking and

Step 1	Step 2	Step 3	Step 4
Facts and Themes	Possible Related Facts and Themes	Possible Major Facts and Themes	Treatment Plan
1. Everything at once	1. Everything at once (major changes)	1. Crisis	1. Focus on one thing at a time
2. Can't cope	–husband sick	–events	2. Relaxation techniques
3. Crying	–fired	–verbal report	3. Very specific and goal directed
4. Became manic/depressive	–change in routines	–behavior	4. Identify strengths and reinforce them
5. Always insecure	2. Husband hospitalized	2. Coping skills	
6. Mo. ago husband blood clot	–renews old fears	3. Connected themes	
7. Went to pieces	–upset family and marital balance	–mother's death and husband's illness	
8. 7-year-old retarded boy	–dependent	–upset in marital balance	
9. No family, only friends	–always insecure		
10. Very dependent	3. No one specific/can't trust		
11. Husband's hospitalization did it	–doctor		
12. Couldn't fix meals	–boss		
13. Not doctor's fault	–husband		
14. Counadin	4. Can't cope		
15. Unlike previous habits	–home		
16. Bruise and swelling	–husband		
17. Two weeks fired	–children		
18. 4 months working/house last year	5. Feels		
19. Spend on self	–alone/fearful		
20. Boss not specific	–treated unfairly		
21. Sensitive person	–vulnerable		
22. Warned two times	–angry (?)		
23. Somatic pains	–guilty		
24. Passed blood/didn't tell	–stability threatened		
25. Mother died of same	6. Strengths		
26. Doctor not specific	–identify stress points		
27. Hitting son	–previous success crisis history		
	–environmental resources		
	–current routines		
	–not psychotic		
	–not dangerous to self/others		

Additional comments:

now it's all caught up with me, and I just can't handle it any more. That's about the size of it. But to really tell you what is wrong, I can't because I don't really know. I just get upset and cry a lot. Thank God my husband understands. He's very understanding.

Part of my problem could be because he has changed jobs so much that it's really upset me and I probably at this point have just reached the point where I can't take any more of it, but I wouldn't leave him. He means too much to me. Now we've worked this out. When he finds a job this time, he won't change any more because Matt has changed. He knows he has done wrong, and he realizes that in his changing jobs he was just searching for something that wasn't there. Now he realizes that, so when he does get a job this time it should solve the problem. Now whether it solves mine or not, I don't know. This remains to be seen. Maybe it will. That might be the whole basis of my problem. Maybe if that was wiped away I wouldn't feel like I do. But I don't know that yet.

I work and right now I don't like my job. I don't like people, and yet I know I can't be alone. I can't stand to be alone. So, I have to have people around me, and yet I get very irritable and upset with them, but I think it's because I'm upset with myself, not with them. I find fault with them because I'm finding fault with myself. Like today. I was going to take the whole day off for a vacation. Well, right away this morning I was upset, wondering what am I going to do with myself? So I was going to go back to work this afternoon. But then my doctor sent me over here and I don't think I'm going to make it, but I do get upset at work too because I'm under quite a bit of pressure, but I've been able to take it up to now. It bothers me at the time but I get over it. I do feel taken advantage of this year, where I didn't before. This one girl is working part time, and I have to do her job as well as my own, which I don't find fair. I don't think it's right, and they've had to bring another in to train because of this and I have to train somebody on my desk, and that has been a good thing because somebody had to learn my job. Up until now nobody has known my job, so I never felt free to take a vacation or anything because nobody knew what I did. This has been good in that sense, because somebody has been forced to learn my job.

I still resent having to do this other girl's work, and she knows how I feel. I told her I didn't like her job and I didn't want to have to do it, but I did. I've stuck with it anyway. I've hurt her feelings and she thought she was losing me as a friend. Well, she hasn't lost me as a friend, but I feel a little taken advantage of by her because some time ago she was using me as a scapegoat to run with a fellow, and I don't appreciate that at all. She's a very nice person and happened to make a mistake and I have no right to judge her, but I am and I shouldn't do it, because she's a very nice woman who happened to make a mistake. I just can't judge her, because she's just not that type. (*Pause.*)

What else? I don't know, maybe if Matt gets a job and everything works out, I may not have to come back here. I hope not. Maybe just talking to you will be enough. But it has been a problem. I've had a bad past which haunts me sometimes, but I realize that I can't look back because I can't undo anything that's already done and even though I had problems before, I know what they were and I've been able to cope with them so far. There's no reason why I can't continue to cope with them. It's just that I've gotten to the point where I can't seem to take any more. That's all. And I don't know what to do about it.

Counselor: How did you handle your problems before?

Client: I just went from day to day battling with them, I guess. That's about all. Probably not solving anything. I've had help before. A doctor that I went to in Ashton gave me hypnosis, which helped immensely, but that was thirteen years ago, and this was before I married again, and I was afraid to get married again. This was the crux of the problem. I realized that I could go on the rest of my life, being afraid to get married again because of what happened to me and I just had to go ahead and try again. And outside of Matt's changing jobs, I couldn't find a better guy. He's been very good to me. So, that's the only complaint I have about him. Sexually, every way, except changing jobs, we get along fine: There has never been any problem that way. Compatability is great and I don't know what else to tell—(*Starts to cry.*)

Counselor: What do you think you are crying about?

Client: I don't know. Probably nothing. When I think about it, I have so much to be thankful for that I don't know why I'm crying really, to tell the truth, because Matt's got a job. It is only temporary, but he has a good job. We don't make enough to live on, but we can get by with both of us working. . . .

Counselor: On your intake you said that you'd had suicidal thoughts since October.

Client: Yes.

Counselor: Could you explain that history?

Client: Well, I have tried suicide before, years ago, with pills . . . they were pain pills, and sleeping pills, and everything I could get my hands on.

Counselor: How old were you then?

Client: About nineteen. Then I tried again a couple of years later when my husband was going to kill me and I was going to do it instead of him. That's why I did it that time. Otherwise, I wouldn't have done that the second time, but it didn't work. I just slept for three or four days most of the time. Nobody knew about it. Nobody knew about the first time I tried it either. I did tell my doctor about it later, and he was a big help to me at the time. I used to be able to go in and talk to him, and he was a big help. . . .

I've been married three times. This is my third marriage and that's probably one reason for the shape I'm in. I think your past has a lot to do with it. The day comes when it all catches up with you, but as far as actually planning any suicide lately, no. I've thought about slitting my wrists, but I'd never have the guts to do it. I'm sure I wouldn't. I'd have to get much worse than I am. If it wasn't for my husband, I probably would do it. (*Voice breaks.*) He keeps me going. (*Starts to cry.*) If I couldn't cry to him and tell him how I feel, I wouldn't make it. I just feel so desperate most of the time and I don't know what to do about it. If I could just get rid of that feeling, but I can't explain it. I can't even tell you what it's like, except that I feel desperate.

Counselor: You were referred by Dr. Reed today?

Client: Yes. Well, he feels that I'm trying to—and I believe he's right— blame the change and not my mental attitude on what's happening to me.

While transcripts cannot capture in its entirety the emotional tone of the interaction between the counselor and the client, they can give the reader a feeling for the introductory elements of an interview. The facts and themes were for the most part subjectively chosen and were selected at the time of the original interview. The reader may choose to select other themes within this organizational plan without necessarily altering the basic approach itself.

Step 1
Facts and Themes

1. Always start crying
2. Don't know problem
3. Change of life
4. Kids left
5. Can't handle any more
6. Husband understands
7. Many job changes, upsetting

8. Unhappy at work
9. Like people, don't
10. Upset with self, not others
11. Doctor referred
12. Contradicts self
13. Upset at work, but managing
14. Cope and can't
15. Previous counseling
16. Previous marriage, fear
17. Husband good, but changes jobs
18. Husband job again
19. Money problem
20. Suicidal history
21. Age and change
22. Married three times
23. Protests too much about husband
24. Doctor says she is blaming change

Next it will be important to identify and discuss several interviewing techniques that will help the counselor gather information about the client's crisis. These techniques will also help introduce the client to the interviewing process, thereby facilitating a positive working relationship between the client and the counselor.

Interviewing Techniques

Achieving Contact

One of the first requirements in the beginning phase of crisis interviewing is to achieve a positive rapport with the client. This starts the moment the counselor begins to get information from the client and continues on throughout the course of counseling. It involves a philosophy of caring about people in trouble and a set of counseling skills, both of which are necessary if one is to achieve a meaningful, helping relationship with the client in crisis.

The importance of achieving contact was suggested by Jones (1968) who defined it as "providing supportive and sympathetic appraisal [of the client's situation] by getting facts [about the crisis]" (1968).

Hamilton discusses the attitude of acceptance as an essential element in counseling. She describes it as

acceptance of the other person as he is in whatever situation, no matter how unpleasant or uncongenial to the interviewer. . . . This attitude can come only from respect for people and a genuine desire to help anyone who is in need or trouble. It is translated through courtesy, patience, willingness to listen and not being critical of whatever the client . . . may reveal about himself (1962).

Fenalson also notes the importance of rapport, pointing out that "the word is used to denote a relationship characterized by harmony and accord" (1962). To Darley rapport is "the prevailing climate that is achieved and maintained throughout the interview." He suggests that "the interviewer should be friendly and interested, appear unhurried and express neither moral or ethical judgment nor approval or disapproval of [the client's] attitudes and ideas" (1946).

Positive rapport is critical in achieving and maintaining contact. It helps establish the foundation necessary to withstand the ensuing stress of crisis counseling. This is particularly true in those instances in which the counselor deals with unusual, bizarre, or unrewarding cases (Rogers 1951).

Finally, Ivey (1971) recognizes that beginning counselors are bound to make a number of communication errors. For example, interrupting the client while he's talking about something important, or asking closed-end questions, or not knowing what to do with long pauses. Many of these errors can be attributed to the fact that the counselor simply doesn't know what to do, since he has had no prior experience in solving such problems.

Ivey suggests several things that the counselor can do to overcome these errors:

In such awkward moments, the interviewer can simply maintain eye contact, retain a relaxed, easy body posture, think back to something that interested him in the client's earlier discussion, make a comment about it, and the interview then can proceed. One of the most important skills that the advanced therapist or personal interviewer has when he feels pressed in the interview is the ability to relax, reflect on the session, and then respond to the client in some appropriate fashion.

Open Invitation to Talk

This technique is often as difficult to practice as it is simple to define. It means that the counselor phrases his questions and comments in a manner that encourages the client to talk freely about his situation. It means avoiding asking closed-end questions that for the most part could be answered by the client with a simple yes or no.

As we have stated, one of the goals in crisis counseling is to get as much information as possible in order to ascertain the nature of the client's crisis. By using open-end questions, particularly when beginning an interview, this can usually be accomplished. It provides plenty of opportunity for the client to begin the interview with what he wants to talk about. Furthermore, an open invitation to talk cuts down on the counselor's talking himself, allowing him more opportunity to listen and to organize what the client is saying. Some examples of the open and closed invitations to talk and their consequences will illustrate this technique.

Open

Counselor: Tell me about yourself!
Client: Well, I'm twenty-nine years old. I have three children and a husband. I live on Denice Hill. I am a native here. Ralph is also a native. We were raised in the area. We are having some problems we can't solve ourselves and we need professional help. . . .

Closed

Counselor: You called in this morning?
Client: Yes.
Counselor: What time was that?
Client: About nine-thirty.

Open

Counselor: Would you start out by telling me your story as you see it?
Client: Well, my husband and I, it started in February, changed very much. I didn't really know what was going on, but anyway at that time he stopped talking to me and just was very cold. He only talked when he had to, and there was not even a touch or anything. We were just living in the same apartment, and it went on like that until just last month, when I found out that he's actually having an affair with another woman, and so he came back one night. He was going to move. . . .

Closed

Counselor: You contacted us Friday for an appointment?
Client: Yes.
Counselor: Dr. B— is your physician. Is he an obstetrician?
Client: Yes.
Counselor: And you have two children?
Client: Yes.
Counselor: What are their names and what are their ages?
Client: Todd and Celeste. Four and two.

In the last example we can see how easy it would be, if the same format were to be followed throughout the interview, for the client to feel as if he were being interviewed for a job or questioned about a crime.

Another difficulty with the closed-end approach is that the counselor may find himself getting the interview off on the wrong foot by teaching the client to wait until he is asked a question before responding, rather than helping the client to respond more freely and spontaneously with his thoughts and feelings. This unfortunate pattern has the added disadvantage of hindering the client's effort to develop informational themes relevant to his crisis situation. This aspect of crisis interviewing is an essential element of the counselor's job. He is to help the client boil the many problems down to their essentials and then offer a plan of action which will hopefully resolve the crisis situation (Jones 1968). To do this with some effectiveness, the counselor must be alert to the themes and try to avoid interfering with their development. Unless specific information is necessary, closed-end questions are best avoided.

Another function of the open-end question is that it begins to provide the client with an idea of the interviewing model the counselor is using, and it tells him how much control the counselor will exercise over the interview. The counselor, then, begins as open-endedly as possible, but as he seeks out new information or clarifies old issues, he may choose to focus in on particular responses, ask closed-end questions, rephrase the client's response, or use other interviewing techniques. The model, however, becomes clear. The counselor is offering only as much structure and control as is necessary to help the client talk about his crisis. The goal is to guide the interview rather than simply let the client talk aimlessly. Heilbrun speaks to this point:

While role expectations for the therapist may encompass a wide range of behaviors, one behavioral dimension which appears to merit priority, as it relates to initial client satisfaction, is the degree of control exerted by the therapist over the conduct of the interview.

As the client enters into his initial contact seeking help for psychological problems, he is likely to expect the professional to bring his training and experience to bear upon the use of his most incisive tool—the interview. To the naive client, interviewer control should call for directive rather than nondirective interview behavior on the part of the counselor (1972).

While we have concentrated on using the open-end question at the beginning of each interview, this does not mean that it cannot be used during other phases of the interview as well. On the contrary, it is an important technique that can be used effectively at various times and will be identified and discussed in future chapters. In similar fashion, while we have discouraged the use of the closed-end question at the beginning of the interview, it too has a very useful place in the interview and will be discussed later on.

For the time being, consider a closed-end question as an appropriate technique to use when the counselor needs some very specific information. Otherwise, try to use facilitating and open-end questions as much as possible.

Bridging Statements

Bridging statements are similar to open-end questions, for they are designed to help the client talk about his crisis. Without intervention from the counselor, the client will often say things that leave the counselor uncertain about the time frame, the place, or the context of the crisis. To help clarify these points, while at the same time not interrupting the process, the counselor may want to insert a word or a phrase, as in the following examples:

Bridging

Client: Well, John really doesn't care if I go somewhere. I'm sure of that. But he says go and then don't go. He wants me to go but he's not secure enough to just let me go. I can understand this part of it. Lately, instead of working with him, I work against him.

Counselor: And when you say lately, what's the time period we're talking about?

Client: Oh, I would say since Christmas. I think probably the biggest reason is because John is unemployed, so we've always had financial stress, and I think this causes a great deal of problems. In fact I know it does. . . .

Another example will illustrate that bridging need not involve more than a couple of words with some voice inflection.

Client: . . . he's got my two little ones upset so this is the reason we took him to the hospital Thursday. His mother is scared. She is scared to be in the house with him.

Counselor: Scared. (*Voice dropping.*)

Client: She is not necessarily scared of being in the room with him. She is at the point right now of being—what would I say?

Client: . . . right now he is unemployed.

Counselor: He's unemployed? (*Voice rising.*)

Client: Well, yeah. He just started getting his unemployment check. In the mail today I got something that shows the different ways you can go to take care of your bills. . . .

One Question At A Time

In the early process of getting information, the counselor will often be tempted to ask more than one question at a time. This is a natural tendency, particularly when the client may be presenting a great deal of information, as occurs in most crisis sessions.

In listening to hours of taped interviews, we have found that if asked a series of questions, the client will often respond by answering the last question in the series and either forget about the others or answer them in an obscure way.

Examples: One Question

Counselor: What caused the divorce?

Client: I didn't like him at all. We got along okay. I don't know if it was because I was so young and didn't know the difference or what. I knew it wasn't really what I thought love was. But, I just stayed with him. . . .

Counselor: What did the drugs do to you?

Client: Nothing. I just didn't like them. I found some weed in my house one time and I literally blew it. I told my sister-in-law . . . I've just always been so scared of drugs. . . .

Examples: Multiple Questions

Counselor: Why did you come to this area? Do you have friends here? Any relatives?

Client: My aunt and uncle, but it's really my boyfriend's aunt and uncle.

Counselor: Have you been served with papers? Are you certain that this is a fact? You can't visit them?

Client: Oh, no! It's not that. I'm sure that he'll even let me visit them. I don't worry about him having them, because I know he'll be good to them. But it's the fact I love them too. . . .

Counselor: Let's return now to the discussion of slugging. Is that something new? It's obviously something you have difficulty in dealing with. Has it gone beyond that?

Client: No. In many areas there's so much that is wonderful between us . . . in this communication bit. It just seems like we fight each other. We're both strong people personality-wise. . . .

Summary

The beginning of a crisis interview sets the tone for the entire interview. Careful beginning preparation requires that the counselor establish personal direction of the interview rather than permit himself to be overcome by the anxious demands of others. The counselor must formulate an over-all picture as to the nature of the crisis by asking himself specific questions detailed in this chapter. It is useful for the counselor to go through a prepared checklist prior to the interview. Brief relaxation techniques are useful, as well. The counselor's initial remarks should remain open-ended, permitting him to direct the interview in accordance with the client's emerging problems. Examples of appropriate and inappropriate openings, derived from actual interviews, are presented.

The goal of every interview is to gather, collect, and organize information about the client's crisis. It is useful for the counselor to develop his short-term memory in search of dominant themes, and to seek answers to relevant questions.

We discussed the usefulness of the deductive model in organizing information and establishing the major themes that run through the interview. The deductive model is an effective framework within which to organize material, and we gave examples of its use with actual interview information.

Finally, we discussed essential interviewing techniques, pointing out the importance of achieving contact, of using openings that invite the client to talk freely, of providing bridging statements to facilitate the interview, and of asking the client in crisis one question at a time.

References

Darley, J. *The Interview in Counseling.* Retraining and Reemployment Administration, U.S. Dept. of Labor, 1946.

Fenalson, A.F., G.B. Ferguson, and A.C. Abrahamson. *Essentials in Interviewing.* New York: Harper & Row, 1962.

Hamilton, G. *Theory and Practice of Social Casework.* New York: Columbia Press, 1962.

Heilbrun, A.B. "Effects of Briefing Upon Client Satisfaction With The Initial Counseling Contact." *Journal of Consulting and Clinical Psychology* 38 (1972): 50.

Ivey, A.E. *Microcounseling: Innovations in Interviewing.* Springfield, Ill.: Charles Thomas, 1971.

Jacobson, E. *You Must Relax.* Chicago: University of Chicago Press, 1934.

Jones, W.L. "The A-B-C Method of Crisis Management." *Mental Hygiene* 52 (1968): 87-89.

Rogers, C.L. *Client-Centered Therapy.* Boston: Houghton Mifflin, 1951.

Sullivan, H.S. *The Psychiatric Interview.* New York: W.W. Norton, 1954.

Wolpe, J. *The Practice of Behavior Therapy.* New York: Pergamon Press, 1969.

Additional Readings

Kadushin, A. *The Social Work Interview.* New York: Columbia University Press, 1972.

MacKinnon, R.A., and R.M. Michels. *The Psychiatric Interview in Clinical Practice.* Philadelphia: W.B. Saunders Co., 1971.

6

The Middle Phase of the Crisis Interview

In many respects the middle phase of the crisis interview is an arbitrary and vaguely defined concept. It has no clearly delineated boundaries as do the beginning and ending stages. Yet tasks and goals accomplished during this period go a long way toward helping the client resolve his crisis state.

The major goal during this phase is the actual problem-solving process, the psychotherapy and counseling aspect of crisis management. The development of this goal, be it during the first interview or subsequent interviews, depends upon several factors: the skill and experience of the counselor, the verbal and conceptual ability of the client, the client's state of mind, the nature and severity of the crisis, the ability of the counselor and client to establish a working relationship, the success of the previous interview, and the state of the counseling process itself.

Crisis counseling as a process should concern itself with both behavior change (public and external data) and the person's inner world (private and internal feelings). In the never ending search for the "necessary and sufficient" conditions underlining this process, Strupp offers the following:

Condition 1
The therapist creates and maintains a helping relationship (patterned in significant respects after the parent-child relationship) characterized by respect, interest, understanding, tact, maturity, and a firm belief in his ability to help.

Condition 2
The foregoing condition provides a power base from which the therapist influences the patient through one or more of the following: (a) suggestions (persuasions); (b) encouragement for openness of communication, self-scrutiny and honesty...; (c) "interpretations" of... self-defeating and harmful strategies in interpersonal relations, ... distorted beliefs about reality, etc.; (d) setting an example of "maturity" and providing a model...; (e) manipulation of rewards (1973).

Condition 3
Both preceding conditions are crucially dependent on a client who has the capacity and willingness to profit from the experience (1973).

To assist in this process, Jacobson, et al., (1965) writing from the psychoanalytic point of view, advocate the following methodological guidelines:

1. active exploration of the current situation in order to identify the precipitating event(s) in the instances where it is not obvious;

67

2. listening for mention of situations in the client's past even symbolically analagous to the current predicament;
3. stating the client's problem to him concisely and in language that he can understand in order to facilitate insight and integration of facts;
4. supporting the client's new efforts at solving his now defined problem and taking a more passive role so that the client can gain self-reliance;
5. avoidance of prolonged discussion of chronic problems; and
6. anticipation of the fact that many clients will not require further professional help after the crisis is resolved.

For additional guidelines the reader is directed to Malan (1963), who emphasizes the "focal technique," and Bellack and Small (1965), who support the psychodynamic approach.

Depending upon such conditions and factors, it may take the counselor a few minutes or a few hours to move into the middle phase, or it may be that there will be times when this is never achieved.

Because we can identify no hard and fast guidelines, we might say, rather facetiously, that the middle phase comprises everything that is left over from the beginning and the ending phase. Crisis counseling, like any form of human interaction, involves certain subjective processes not amenable to objective modes of knowledge. Strupp states that this aspect of the art of psychotherapy "consists of knowing when and how to communicate interest, respect, understanding, empathy, etc. . . . and when not to" (1973). The outstanding crisis counselor, then, must learn to master his technical skills so that he may practice this human art all the more effectively.

Interviewing Techniques

The following interviewing techniques are designed to facilitate and enhance the effectiveness of the middle phase. However, they may be employed at any time. They may be used in the beginning, middle or ending phase, with the single- or multiple-session interview. They may be used sparingly or repeatedly, depending upon the needs of the situation. Whichever the case, they are another set of technical skills designed to promote a better grasp of the client's crisis state and its subsequent resolution.

"Earlier You Said"

This phrase can be used by the counselor whenever he wishes to return to something the client mentioned in a previous part of the interview. The phrase, when presented at the end of a client's sentence or when there is a long pause, can signal the counselor's intentions to the client. This cue then lets the client know that the counselor has something specific in mind, and that some structure is being introduced into the process. When he conducts the interview in this way, the counselor interferes minimally with what the client is communicating, and the process of "talking about what the client wants" is not seriously disrupted. Yet this particular question lets the client know that their talking together has some definite purpose. By asking questions without interrogating, the counselor smoothly yet effectively focuses on precisely what it is that he wants to talk about.

Example

Counselor: Earlier you said: "I have had thoughts of suicide." Can you describe those to me?

Client: I can remember times in my life when I would have, but I always found an excuse. . . . I don't know. The one time that I really came close was when my sister died and I found out that my husband was cheating on me. . . .

"Earlier You Talked About"

This is a slight modification of the previous technique. The difference here is in the wording: *talked about* rather than *said*. With this slight change the counselor is presenting a more open-ended invitation to explore content and feelings. This phrasing can be used to examine a broader topic area, or it can be substituted in case the counselor has forgotten the specifics of what the client had said.

Example

Counselor: Earlier you talked about your father. What would you say your relationship was with him?

Client: I've been thinking about that. . . .

"Tell Me About That"

With general and ambiguous statements such as "I'm depressed," "They hate me," "I feel upset" or "They are always fighting," the counselor will want to get a more specific definition of just what the client is talking about. Though these and similar phrases can be clarified any time during the interview, we place them in the middle phase. We do this so as not to interfere too early with the client's developing his story as he feels it. The person in crisis will frequently want to talk, or at least have the opportunity to talk, without too much interference from the counselor. Thus, the sensitive counselor will try to wait until the middle phase before he focuses too much effort on clarifying some of the crisis themes. The indirect question technique can also be useful when the client has offered a statement hinting at his desire to be encouraged to continue talking.

Examples

Client:	. . . you know it just makes me feel so bad.
Counselor:	Tell me about that.
Client:	Well, it's kind of hard to explain, but it just seems to come over me with not much warning. . . .

Counselor:	. . . You just mentioned you had been dragged into family problems. Tell me about that.
Client:	A couple of years back, in my junior year, my parents got divorced. She got a job and then I had the whole responsibility of keeping up the house and watching my brother and sister. . . .

We see in the first example how the client may offer a closed-end, yet vague statement. The counselor responds with a comment that is designed to achieve a better understanding of what the client means. Far too often, we see clients and counselors interacting as if each knows what the other means when certain descriptive statements are used, when in reality neither party understands the other.

"What Do You Do When . . . ?"

This question is designed to help make an assessment of how the person in crisis deals with potentially upsetting material and provides the counselor with insight as to how the client responds to various stress situations. This question assists in formulating some idea of the client's behavioral repertoire, his mental status, his impulse control, his way of perceiving certain stimulus situations, the ways in which he *might* be expected to handle future situations, and his emotional reactions to them.

Example

Counselor:	What do you do when you get really afraid?
Client:	Well, I run away.

Counselor:	What do you do when he says that?
Client:	I really get angry and I want to lash out at them. I don't. I'm a chicken.

"Can You Summarize?"

This most useful question can be employed at almost any time during the crisis interview, but it can be particularly helpful during the middle and ending phases. By the time the interview has progressed beyond five or ten minutes, there is likely to be a great deal of information facing the counselor. What better way of saying "Halt" without interfering too much with the client's narrative than by asking the client to summarize some of the things he's said? For that matter, the counselor may want to institute this procedure specifically to review pertinent information.

Example

Counselor: So far you have presented a great deal of information. Could we pause a moment, so I could summarize?
Client: Sure, go ahead.

Counselor: We've talked about a lot of problems, could you please summarize some of them;
Client: Well, I'll try. . . .

Summarization, if used thoughtfully, can be a useful technique, enabling both client and counselor to reestablish a perspective regarding the course of counseling. Oftentimes, with so much feeling and content emerging from a crisis counseling experience, all participants can lose perspective on what is happening to them, thus interfering with the rapid development of practicable courses of action.

Silence

While silence is not a questioning technique in the strict sense of the word, it certainly can be used in that way, and plays an important role during the middle phase of the interviewing process. Silence is the deliberate withholding of speech. It is unlike a pause, which is considered a "natural resting place" in the process of speech. Among other things, it is designed to help the client organize his thoughts and feelings and to review what has transpired during the counseling experience. For the counselor, it is helpful in assisting him to formulate and integrate what he has heard and observed so far. It is a communicative gesture that has multiple meanings (Cook 1964; Fliess 1949; Jarrett 1966; Weisman 1955; Kadushian 1972).

Wolberg offers an outline of how the counselor might handle client silences that are longer than five seconds (1954). Some of his suggestions include: saying "hmmmm" or "I see," and then waiting for a moment; saying "And?" or "But?" with a questioning emphasis, as if something else is to follow; or the counselor may say, "You find it difficult to talk" or "It's hard to talk." In the event of no reply, then: "I wonder why you are so silent?"

Some additional questions that may assist the counselor during this phase are:

1. "How long has this been going on?"
2. "What were the circumstances surrounding that situation?"
3. "Has anything like this happened before?"
4. "What have you been able to do about this?"
5. "A point of clarification. . . ."
6. "I would like to hear what you have to say/think/feel."

As mentioned, none of the techniques presented so far need be restricted only to the middle phase. On the contrary, they have broad application and should be inserted whenever they will facilitate the process of effective crisis resolution.

Middle Phase—First Interview

In the first interview, it can be said that the middle phase of crisis interviewing occurs when the counselor is able to identify some of the major themes that begin to develop as the client talks about his situation. It is the time when the material that has been presented begins to make some clinical sense to the counselor, and he begins to gain a clearer picture of what has produced this crisis. It is the time when many of the questions identified in Chapter 5 begin to be answered. It is also the time when the counselor should be prepared to clarify some of the issues that have emerged in the initial phase of the interview. This stage develops further as the counselor and client begin to see connections among the themes of the crisis state and how they relate to the current situation.

In the presentation of our deductive model, we have outlined several steps in the process of organizing the material of a crisis interview. For descriptive purposes, we would say that steps 2 and 3 comprise the middle phase in this initial interview.

The Single Session

There will be instances where the single crisis contact will be the only opportunity the counselor will have to affect some kind of crisis resolution. Within this limited amount of time, then, the counselor should keep his goals and expectations realistic and reasonable. Basic personality changes with severe and chronic problems are simply not going to occur in an hour or two of crisis counseling. It is more likely that only the more pressing and immediately accessible and resolvable problems can be identified and dealt with. In these instances, the counselor should be prepared to take a much more active role in the utilization of the techniques outlined in Chapter 4.

While there is increased utilization of the single-session interview in police domestic work (Schwartz and Liebman 1972) and hospital emergency rooms, (Getz, Fujita, and Allen 1974), this is not to be construed as a substitute for the more extended crisis contacts involving multiple sessions.

In such instances the counselor should keep his expectations realistic given (1) the amount of time he has with the client, (2) the nature of the crisis, (3) the counselor's skill and background, (4) the client's expectations and goals, and (5) the institutional setting of the crisis service.

Unanswered Questions

In Chapter 5 we outlined some fourteen questions that the counselor needs answers to in order to establish an effective treatment plan. During the middle phase of this first interview, the counselor can guide and direct the interview so as to get answers to these questions. For the client, this phase can be a time in which he is given a free opportunity to express himself in regard to these and other related questions. The emphasis here is upon a thorough and exhaustive exploration of all that is important to both parties. The message that the counselor conveys, then, is one of attention to, and a deep sense of respect for, the client's state of mind. This approach is bound to have a positive effect on the counseling process. It will strengthen the client's perception that the counselor is a helping person. And out of this relationship should emerge an effective plan that will help resolve the crisis.

Another important element to consider during this phase is the idea that the participants will be getting to know one another better. McKinnon and Michels (1971) observe that one such question for the counselor to raise is: "What sort of person are you?" This may be expressed out loud or retained in the counselor's head. Either way, this question has both "achieving contact" value and clinical usefulness. Clinically, the counselor could be performing some aspects of his mental status examination (see Appendix C). Also, the counselor would be understanding how, in certain situations, the client may see himself in quite a different light than he normally would, owing to the circumstances of his crisis. This type of inquiry may be used later to help the client regain some of his lost equilibrium. It will certainly help the counselor gain some idea of the client's self-perception, his strengths and weaknesses, how he was functioning before the crisis, and perhaps some idea of immediate and long-range personal goals.

Furthermore, the counselor may unearth some more relevant information concerning the client's feelings about asking for help. Since our culture presents ambivalent values about asking for help with personal problems, the manner in which this area is dealt with may have some effect upon the success of the counseling process itself (Winder 1962). This ambivalence regarding "help-seeking" behavior apparently has something to do with missed appointments and early termination (Mendelson and Geller 1967).

Middle Phase—Subsequent Interviews

During the initial interview the emphasis was upon gathering information, assessing the client's crisis state, trying to establish a climate of positive regard, formulating the many themes into a workable intervention plan, and then initiating some kind of problem-solving process. At this point the counselor was setting the stage for the middle phase of subsequent sessions as well. As mentioned, the major goal during this phase is to participate with the client in a crisis-resolution plan.

This middle phase may be called the "essence" of the counseling process. During this phase the counselor will use his skills as a therapist to bring about some clearer understanding of the forces that have contributed to the client's current situation. But more than that, it is the time when the participants are actively engaged in pursuing avenues of crisis resolution. This phase often evokes complex and sometimes anxiety-producing states for both the counselor and client.

Some Common Themes

In a series of articles Howard, Orlansky, and Hill have isolated some of the themes that clients have identified as meaningful during the therapeutic process. In the first article (1969), based upon the reports of female clients in an outpatient setting, the following topics were most frequently mentioned: relations with the opposite sex, hopes or fears about the future, work, career or education, and mother. In another study (1968), clients reported the following topics to be of concern: personal identity, self-disclosure, responsibilities, loneliness, loving, and anger. In another study (1970), clients reported feeling: serious, accepted, anxious, confident, relaxed, hopeful, confused, determined, relieved, grateful, likable, pleased, frustrated, and inadequate. To the best of our knowledge, there has been no research designed to specifically isolate the feelings and content material of clients who are seen in crisis.

It has been our observation, though, that the themes are similar. However, we would add that in crisis work the counselor is much more likely to encounter the extremes of disturbing behavior and intense feelings.

Additional Considerations

During the middle stage of the crisis-resolution process, the counselor will often employ several of the intervention techniques that are most common to all psychotherapeutic interventions, some of which have been outlined in Chapter 4. These will include such techniques as: confrontation, counterconditioning techniques, and role rehearsal and modeling. In addition, offering support and encouragement, establishing a sense of hope in this demoralizing dilemma, and considering plans for resolution are equally important facets of this phase (Frank 1972).

The middle phase should be the period in which the counseling process moves toward an effective resolution and termination of the crisis state. In all likelihood the speed with which the client and counselor move into the middle phase will differ from one session to the next, and it is also probable that there will be a different tempo and flow from session to session depending on what has transpired in previous sessions, as well as what has happened in the client's life since the counselor last saw him.

Throughout the middle phase the counselor must remain flexible and be prepared to deal with anything that comes up. Due to space limitations, we have outlined only some of the factors that a counselor may be expected to consider. The techniques, while clear and concise, may not always work as smoothly as we have presented them. However, they are necessary additions to a crisis counselor's repertoire and should be used and modified as the situation requires.

Summary

The middle phase of the crisis interview is not easily defined and may be subjectively determined. During this phase, however, the crisis counselor goes beyond the routine collection of information and attempts to conceptualize, with the client, the various aspects of the crisis state.

We gave specific examples of questions that can be useful in eliciting various types of information from the client. Among these questions are: "What do you do when . . . ?" and "Earlier you said . . . " "Can you summarize?"

We examined some of the common themes and feeling states and discussed guidelines for dealing with the crisis situation.

We also noted several interviewing and psychotherapy techniques useful in promoting rapid resolution of crisis.

References

Bellak, L., and L. Small. *Emergency Psychotherapy and Brief Psychotherapy.* New York: Grune & Stratton, 1965.

Cook, J.J. "Silence in Psychotherapy." *Journal of Counseling Psychology* 11 (1964): 42-46.

Fliess, R. "Silence and Verbalization." *International Journal of Psychoanalysis* 30 (1949): 21-30.

Frank, J. "The Bewildering World of Psychotherapy." *Journal of Social Issues* 28 (1972): 27-43.

Getz, W., B. Fujita and D. Allen. "The Use of Paraprofessionals In Crisis Intervention: The Evaluation Of An Innovative Program. Accepted for publication, *American Journal of Community Psychology*, 1974.

Howard, K.I., D.E. Orlinsky, and J.A. Hill. "Content of Dialogue In Psychotherapy." *Journal of Counseling Psychology* 16 (1969); 396-404.

————. "Affective Experience In Psychotherapy" *Journal of Abnormal Psychology* 75 (1970): 267-75.

Jacobson, G. "Crisis Theory and Treatment Strategy: Some Sociocultural and Psychodynamic Considerations." *Journal of Nervous and Mental Disease* 141 (1965): 209-18.

Jarrett, F.J. "Silence in Psychiatric Interviews." *British Journal of Medical Psychology* 39 (1966): 357-62.

Kadushin, A. *The Social Work Interview*. New York: Columbia University Press, 1972.

MacKinnon, R.A., and R. Michels. *The Psychiatric Interview in Clinical Practice*. Philadelphia: W.B. Saunders Co., 1971.

Malan, D.H. *A Study of Brief Psychotherapy*. London: Tavistock Publications, 1963.

Mendelsohn, G., and M. Geller. "Similarity, Missed Sessions, and Early Termination." *Journal of Counseling Psychology* 14 (1067): 210-15.

Orlinsky, D.E., and K.I. Howard. "The Good Therapy Hour." *Archives of General Psychiatry* 16 (1967): 621-32.

Strupp, H.H. "On The Basic Ingredients of Psychotherapy." *Journal of Counseling and Clinical Psychology* 41 (1973): 1-18.

Wolberg, L.R. *The Technique of Psychotherapy*. New York: Grune & Stratton, 1974.

Schwartz, J.A., and D.A. Liebman. "Police Programs in Domestic Crisis Intervention: A Review." In *The Urban Police in Transition*. (Eds. Snibbe and Snibbe.) C.C. Thomas and Sons, 1973.

Weisman, A. "Silence and Psychotherapy." *Psychiatry* 18 (1955): 241-60.

Winder, C.I., Z.A. Farrukh, B. Bandura, and L.C. Rau. "Dependency of Patients, Psychotherapist's Responses, and Aspects of Psychotherapy." *Journal of Counseling Psychology* 26 (1962): 129-34.

7

The Ending Phase of the Crisis Interview

Several tasks should be accomplished during the ending phase. In the first place, it is the logical opportunity to bring together many of the problem areas that have been defined as sources of psychological or social dysfunction during the session. Second, it is the time to assist the client in achieving relevant and workable solutions. Third, a crisis resolution plan is developed and goals for the next counseling session are formulated. Fourth, the client and counselor should have an opportunity to review and assess the process of the specific interview and of the counseling process to date. Fifth, it will be the time when the client and counselor will be saying goodby until the next session—unless of course, the crisis has been resolved. This phase is step 4 of the deductive model in Chapter 5.

Ending Phase—First Interview

In practical terms, how are these goals to be accomplished? As mentioned, the counselor will want to pull the themes together into an organized picture. In crisis work, it is not unusual to be faced with as many as twenty to thirty informational themes. Thus, it becomes quite a problem to decide which are the most important and which are not. To help deal with this issue, we propose that the problem-identification process should be clearly stated and shared between client and counselor. To accomplish this, the counselor should ask the client to state the first, second, and third most significant problems that offer the best possibility of solution. This approach has several advantages. It says to the client that he is an active participant in the crisis resolution process. It says that he has something to say about countering the forces that have brought him into crisis. And it implies that he is responsible for his role in seeking a solution. This participation as a way out of the demoralizing dilemma may have considerable therapeutic value (Frank 1972). Further, it establishes expectations for the entire counseling contract and undoubtedly influences subsequent interviews.

Another feature of this participatory approach is that no one person in the therapeutic transaction can take all of the credit or all of the blame. While the very nature of the situation implies that one person has more expertise than the other, this need not always be exploited. And this is particularly true during the terminating phase of the crisis interview.

Example

Counselor: We have discussed a number of things during this interview. Could we perhaps pull some of these together by having you list the number 1, 2, and 3 things that you consider the most important ones?

Client: Well . . . first I want to do something about my mother-in-law. She is the main problem. Then, I guess . . . my job. And I don't know what would be third.

Counselor: Mr. Jones, what would you say were your number 1, 2, and 3 problems that we could work on to help you out of your crisis?

Client: I don't know for sure. That is why I'm here. But if I have to make a choice, it would be my wife's spending first, and then her nagging about my going fishing. . . .

It is not always possible nor desirable to follow this approach. Some notable exceptions would be those persons who are so disturbed that their ability to make coherent decisions is impaired. This would include severely suicidal and homicidal clients, psychotics, clients requiring hospitalization where there is no choice, and severe mental retardation.

When the counselor is presented with the client's perception of what problem areas the client feels of highest priority, the counselor should not assume a passive stance. On the contrary, he should bring to bear all of his skills and experience in helping the client focus on items that are likely to have some impact on resolving the crisis. Of particular importance is the idea that whatever problems the client chooses to deal with, the counselor is responsible for enhancing his client's probability of success. Even small successes increase the client's confidence in his own resources at a time when such confidence is urgently needed.

Success Leads to Success

In an interesting study by Cohen and Walder (1971), the researchers simulated several crisis situations and then exposed groups of children to two variables: success and failure in mastering crisis situations of various degrees of severity. The researchers concluded that two major elements influence the effectiveness or ineffectiveness with which one will cope with present and future crisis situations. They state: "The present research has shown that opportunity to cope, and successful coping in crises that gradually increase in severity, are important for success in future coping." Therefore, the extent of the client's previous coping history and the severity of the current crisis should be carefully considered before determining which of the client's problems to address first.

Occasionally the client may choose to address some problem that has little or no possibility of immediate resolution. The client then is faced with the prospect of feeling even more helpless and frustrated, and this may only further the client's state of crisis. The counselor can assist in reducing this destructive process by stating to the client the importance of dealing with problems that offer reasonable chances of success. The counselor should be aware that in this approach of mutual goal setting, there are very real possibilities that the client will choose inappropriate problems. This may be due to unconscious motivation to fail, poor judgment, or even deliberate sabotage. At such times the counselor's skill can play an important role. He will want to help the client see what he is doing in the selection of the problems and use such techniques as confrontation, reflection, and interpretation to help in this endeavor.

In general, then, the counselor will do well to urge the client to choose his priorities realistically, from among those that offer a high probability of success. Specifically, he may support the client's attempts to deal with such practical matters as getting dinner prepared on time, getting to work regularly, openly expressing his previously suppressed feelings to someone else. This will give the client an immediate opportunity to see that the outcome of his efforts has had some impact. Then the counselor can reinforce his progress and strengthen still further the client's emerging adaptive responses to what seemed before to be an impossible situation.

Examples

1. A mother with multiple family problems identifies the temper tantrums of her four-year-old son as her major problem. She complains that her son provokes her anger to the extent that she is afraid she will lose control and beat him. The counselor provides her with some reading material emphasizing an approach that could have an immediate effect on her relationship with her son and consequently on his behavior problem; e.g., G. Patterson and E. Gullion, *Living with Children*; M. Meacham and A. Wiesen, *Changing Classroom Behavior.*

2. A middle-aged man who complains of always feeling tense and anxious may be offered some muscular-relaxation training. As part of this approach the counselor would recommend E. Jacobson's book *You Must Relax.* It would give the client something to work on immediately and elevate his hopes. If appropriate, the counselor could set aside some time during the interview and give him some exercises in this method.

3. A couple whose primary problem entails marital fights and arguments that have reached crisis proportions may be referred to G. Bach's, *The Intimate Enemy.*

This use of reading material as a therapeutic technique is just another addition to the counselor's repertoire. It is not designed to replace other counseling techniques.

Once the highest priority problems have been identified, we advise the crisis counselor to encourage the client to be as specific as possible in addressing them. The following interviewing technique may be helpful in this respect, a technique that Jones calls "boiling the problems down to their essentials" (1968).

Focusing

This technique can be used whenever the counselor needs some very specific information. It goes hand in hand with the closed-end question except that it is a concept rather than a question, whose only answer is a yes or no response. Its purpose is to narrow things down so that the counselor and client will be able to focus upon certain subject matters. It should be introduced after the client completes his or her sentence. In some instances it will be necessary to interrupt a rambling client, particularly if the counselor starts to hear a repetition of themes. But for the most part, it is best to wait until the client has completed his thought before introducing the focusing comment. Some examples of this technique include: "How does that strike you?" or "Does that make sense?" Frequently the client will stop once he has broadly defined his problem and feelings. Usually this does not provide sufficient information. Therefore, the more specific and precise the counselor and client can be, the more effective they can be in developing an effective crisis resolution plan.

The Time Factor

The ending phase of the first interview should take up as much time as the client and counselor feel is necessary. Unlike subsequent interviews, time may not be as pressing an issue. That is, the counselor may wish to avoid a feeling of time urgency by purposely not scheduling an interview with another client immediately following his new client's first interview. Because initial interviews vary in length, it is best to provide more than enough time for the first session.

Another consideration is that this is the first time the counselor and client have met. The amount of information that the counselor will be required to assimilate and deal with can be quite overwhelming. Thus, in the ending phase of the first contact, the counselor may want to take some extra time to clarify the treatment program. A little extra time at this juncture of the crisis contact may pay rich dividends later in terms of a more rapid over-all resolution of the client's crisis.

While it is difficult to make a sweeping generalization concerning how much time to set aside for the ending phase, the counselor should remain aware of the time and allow a minimum of ten minutes. The client's frame of mind, the extent of the crisis, the number of persons being interviewed regarding this crisis, and the amount of tangible and emotional stresses evoked by the situation will determine the amount of time the counselor devotes to this phase. In those instances in which there is another client waiting to keep a previously established appointment, the counselor should feel it appropriate to excuse himself for a moment to tell the client who is waiting that it will be another few minutes. This can be quite helpful to all concerned, particularly to the counselor, since it will relieve him of the anxiety that he must hurry or a feeling of guilt in neglecting his next client. Because the counselor is then freed to concentrate his full attention upon the client before him, both client and counselor can be expected to benefit significantly from this tactic.

Ending Phase—Subsequent Interviews

In those instances in which the counselor has an opportunity to work with the client for more than one session, some general guidelines need to be considered. Many of the principles that have been spelled out in regard to the ending phase of the single interview will be applicable to all subsequent interviews as well. However, sometimes modification is necessary owing to the length of the time interval between sessions, a change of the client's status, and a host of other variables.

The ending phase of subsequent interviews should feature a clear outlining of the goals and tasks to be accomplished before the next session. The specifics of the work that has been agreed upon should be clear to both client and counselor. Here is where a summary can be of significant help. The purpose is to provide a sense of continuity and focus from one interview to the next. Unlike noncrisis-oriented counseling, the counselor cannot afford the luxury of taking a *laissez faire* approach, nor would such an approach be an appropriate therapeutic technique in crisis work. The work is goal-oriented, with emphasis on rapid resolution of the presenting problems. For those who need and want additional psychotherapy, referral is surely the most appropriate procedure.

The ending phase of subsequent interviews may take just a few minutes with summary, or many minutes with direct focusing. In those instances in which the client may be overwhelmed by the amount of material covered during the session, the counselor should make a deliberate effort to begin the ending phase earlier than he normally would. This same principle should be put into effect in every instance in which it appears that the client is obviously distraught and overloaded with crisis material. Thus, it is not appropriate for either counselor or client to introduce new material just prior to the end of the interview. In those sessions in which several items are brought up, it may be helpful for the counselor or client to write them down so that they will not be forgotten by the next session.

The ending phase may be used as a time to review what has taken place during the session. Furthermore, it is sometimes wise to identify specifically some of the main issues. This should be a joint counselor/client task, with the emphasis upon clarification. The counselor should be ready to reiterate material that might facilitate crisis resolution. For the client, the ending phase is an opportunity to be specific about what he or she considers to have been the important and meaningful points of the session. It further provides a potential feedback experience to correct distortions for both client and counselor, and it may also serve to aid retention of important information.

Another function of the ending phase is to learn if there is any other material that may need to be discussed. This is not in contradiction to what we said earlier, however. The counselor should be paying attention to what has been said during the middle phases and use the ending phase to tie together any potentially loose ends that he felt were not dealt with earlier. This requires a degree of skill on the part of the counselor so as not to introduce extraneous or explosive material so near the end. In clinical circles it is often reported that the last few minutes of the session are the most meaningful. Regardless of the truth of this belief, it will be important to use this time appropriately. It may be that the client will want to prolong the interview for such reasons as: the client's hostility, his avoidance of important material, his reluctance to share the counselor with the next client, etc. (Kadushin 1972). These issues can be effectively discussed in the ending phase or during a subsequent interview.

In general then, the counselor will need to bring the interview to a close without prematurely closing off the communication so abruptly that it offends the client. In our culture, separation is often confused with personal rejection, and unless clarified, the client might leave the interview with this impression. While it is not always possible to tie all the loose ends together before closing an interview, the counselor should always make the attempt. As Kadushin (1972) states: "The interviewee should be emotionally at ease when the interview is terminated."

Examples

"In the few remaining minutes of this session . . . ."

"We have to stop in a few minutes, would you like to summarize . . . ?"

"That is important material, but we will have to wait and get into that next session."

Once the counselor has stated his intention, he should, as a rule, stick with it. There are unusual exceptions, of course, that would require continuing the contact, such as significant suicidal or homicidal material. But in the main, the interview should be limited to the agreed upon period of time.

The following outline is designed to help both the counselor and client organize the key elements of the crisis in preparation for the next session. As noted, it provides a quick review of the client's current status, the status of the intervention plan, new information, and the plan and goals for the next session. This organization format can be expected to reduce the tendency to stray from important goals, thus saving time and minimizing confusion regarding past, present, or future goals. Furthermore, it indicates the degree of progress or lack of it in the counseling process. The goal of crisis work is, to a large extent, culturally determined. However, generally speaking it is to help the client reestablish a definite sense of mastery over his crisis state and gain a sense of self-control (Bergin and Strupp 1972). By pointing out progress that has been made, and how it was accomplished, the counselor helps the client get a clearer picture of the resources he can draw upon to deal with future crisis.

If the counselor feels that it is inappropriate to go into as much detail as we have outlined in the above model, the counselor and client can review the topical

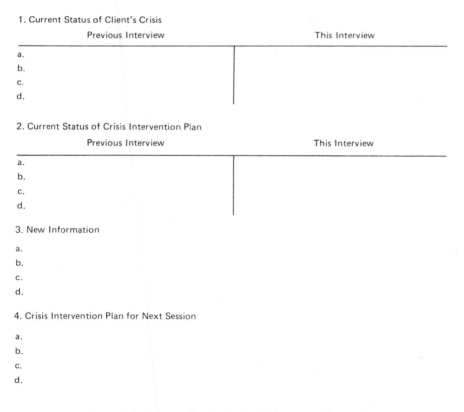

1. Current Status of Client's Crisis

    Previous Interview   This Interview

a.
b.
c.
d.

2. Current Status of Crisis Intervention Plan

    Previous Interview   This Interview

a.
b.
c.
d.

3. New Information

a.
b.
c.
d.

4. Crisis Intervention Plan for Next Session

a.
b.
c.
d.

Figure 7-1. Format for Outlining Subsequent Interviews

headings verbally. In either case, the competent counselor attempts to be as clear as possible in regard to what has transpired during the counseling process, and regarding what is expected of the client by the next interview. Crisis intervention is a goal-directed activity, occurring within a limited span of time. Therefore, the counselor must of necessity be more direct and concrete in outlining a crisis resolution plan. Whatever the specific format of the session, it is important that the counselor remain flexible in his approach. There are always exceptions and situations that simply will not fit the proposed model. As always, the effective counselor must be prepared to adapt his approach to the needs of his clients.

Ending Phase—Last Interview

It has always been easier to say hello than goodby. Little in our culture prepares us to engage in this activity. Therefore, it should not surprise the crisis counselor to find that he will run into certain difficulties when he attempts to do this with clients. How many times have clinicians experienced the frustration of not being able to say goodby to their clients because the clients fail to show up for the last appointment? What of the client who simply stops coming because he anticipates this painful process? And how can the counselor deal with the client who simply denies that he has any feelings at all about saying goodby? Only infrequently will a counselor meet a client who will persevere to this phase of the crisis resolution process. And that is a shame, because saying goodby is the inevitable consequence of saying hello, and there is much growth potential inherent in this experience, as painful as it sometimes is.

When it becomes clear that the goals of the crisis work are being accomplished and that termination is close, the counselor should be prepared to disengage. If the client does not introduce the idea, then the counselor should. With crisis work the significance of saying goodby is made implicit by the transitory nature of the crisis and the minimal number of visits. Kubler-Ross in her book, *On Death and Dying*, provides an excellent exposure to this element of the counseling process and should be helpful in furthering an understanding of both client's and counselor's feelings.

Client-Counselor Feelings

Just because the period of time in which counselor and client are together is relatively brief does not diminish in any way the intensity of the experience for the participants. O'Connell describes crisis work as a "walk through hell" (1970). While this may be exaggerated, it does convey some of the potential impact that the crisis counseling process can have on both client and counselor. It is often helpful to verbalize this struggle in hopes of dealing with it in a more constructive way.

The Client

In the first place, if the counseling process has been a positive one and the client-counselor relationship has been warm, the client may be quite reluctant to give it up. Therefore, rather than having to face the many feelings likely to be evoked at the thought of termination, it becomes easier to avoid that process by never dealing with it openly. Another possibility is that the client may be angry at the counselor or otherwise dissatisfied with the counseling relationship. One way of expressing that displeasure is to terminate without closure. Yet another possibility is that the counselor has never made it clear that termination can be a growth-promoting experience, not merely a painful one. At times, of course, the client's failure to remain in counseling until a satisfactory resolution is reached is nothing more than a further indication of the client's destructive or self-destructive pattern of life. But a consistent pattern of premature client termination must lead the counselor to seriously reconsider the way in which he is coming across to his clients. In psychoanalytic terms this might be called the counselor's "countertransference problems."

The Counselor

The counselor has had more exposure to the termination process and is in a somewhat better position to deal with it than the client. This, however, is not necessarily sufficient to ensure that the counselor will handle this phase appropriately. Some of the very things that hinder the client's termination process apply equally to the counselor. But, in addition, there are other aspects. The counselor has a lot of investment in the successful resolution of the client's crisis state. For example, if it has been going poorly and the counselor knows it, he may not want to terminate when it is apparent he should. It is difficult to face a client and suggest termination when it is clear that the client thinks poorly of the counselor's performance.

Conversely, another problem occurs when the counselor has really enjoyed the client's successful experience and has a certain reluctance to give it up. Saying goodby to something that feels good is usually difficult. Another feature may be that in the counselor's opinion termination is premature; the agreed upon goals were not achieved. Dealing with the frustration of this situation then becomes an important consideration in this termination process.

Saying Goodby

Some questions that are appropriate for the counselor to ask are: "How do you feel about terminating?" "What do you think about saying goodby?" "What kind of feelings do you have?" Often it will be helpful if the counselor inquires about what kinds of previous experiences the client has had with this event. Thus, the counselor has some idea of how the client may handle the present termination. This historical material may have already emerged during the beginning or middle phase, but it is always helpful to clarify it in this part of the interview. If the client has some difficulty in formulating his ideas and feelings, then the counselor may very appropriately talk about some of his own feelings in order to serve as a model for the client. Of course, in the process of self-disclosure, the counselor may be working out some of his own conflicts about saying goodby too. This is appropriate only to the degree that it is not conducted at the expense of the client.

There is no iron rule about how to say goodby. Sometimes a handshake, a smile, and friendly words will suffice. At other times a warm embrace may be indicated. Whatever the form of expression, it should be genuine and sincere. To terminate on a sour note has a dampening effect on the whole goodby experience, an outcome we hope to avoid.

How much time should be set aside for saying goodby is difficult, if not impossible, to say. It all depends. It may take a few seconds, several minutes, or longer. By and large, the perceptive counselor will have a pretty good idea by now of how his client will respond to termination and should gear his time accordingly. If the counselor has been paying close attention to such factors as the counseling process, his own state of mind, the client's history regarding dependency and termination, then saying goodby will occur as a natural experience. Under those conditions there should not be too many surprises.

Summary

The ending phase of the crisis interview requires a bringing together of relevant aspects of what has transpired in counseling. We discussed the importance of summarization during this phase and noted such techniques as focusing, reviewing precisely what has been accomplished, and what will be done in subsequent sessions.

We pointed out that the time limitations inherent in crisis counseling often require that the counselor be more directed than he might be in longer-term counseling. We also discussed the benefits of obtaining feedback from the client in regard to his feelings about the session.

Finally, we discussed the difficulties that may ensue when it is time to say goodby. Constructive termination may be hampered by either or both client and counselor for such reasons as an inability to face separation, or the desire to express dissatisfaction with the relationship between client and counselor.

References

Bach, G., and P. Widen. *The Intimate Enemy*. New York: Wm. Morrow Co., 1968.

Bergin, A.E., and H.H. Strupp. *Changing Frontiers In The Science of Psychotherapy.* Chicago, Aldine-Atherton, 1972.

Cohen, S., and L. Walder. "An Experimental Analog Derived From Crisis Theory." *American Journal Orthopsychiatry* 41 (1971): 822-29.

Frank, J. "The Bewildering World of Psychotherapy." *Journal of Social Issues* 28 (1972): 27-43.

Jones, W.L. "The A-B-C Method of Crisis Management." *Mental Hygiene* 52 (1968): 87-89.

Kadushin, A. *The Social Work Interview.* New York: Columbia University Press, 1972.

Kubler-Ross, E. *On Death & Dying.* New York: The Macmillan Company, 1969.

Meacham, M., and A. Wiesen. *Changing Classroom Behavior.* Scranton, Pa.: International Textbook Co., 1969.

O'Connell, V.F. "Crisis Psychotherapy; Person Dialogue, and the Organismic Event." In *Gestalt Therapy Now.* (Eds. J. Fagen, and I.L. Shepherd.) New York: Harper & Row, 1970.

Patterson, G., and E. Gullian. *Living With Children.* Champaign, Ill.: Research Press, 1968.

Suggested Readings

Aldrich, C.K. "Brief Psychotherapy: A Reappraisal of Some Theoretical Assumptions." *American Journal of Psychiatry* 125 (1968): 585-92.

Deutsch, F., and W.F. Murphy. *The Clinical Interview.* Vols. 1 and 2. New York: International University Press, 1955.

Garrett, A.M. *Interviewing: Its Principles & Methods.* New York: Family Welfare Association of America, 1942.

Jacobson, E. *You Must Relax.* Chicago: University of Chicago Press, 1934.

Miller, L.C. "Short-Term Therapy with Adolescents." In *Crisis Intervention: Selected Readings* (Ed. H.J. Parad). New York: Family Service Association of America, 1965.

Sifneos, P.E. "Two Different Kinds of Psychotherapy of Short Duration." *American Journal of Psychiatry* 123 (1967): 1069.

Wolberg, L.R. "The Technique of Short-Term Psychotherapy." In *Short-term Psychotherapy* (Ed. L.R. Wolberg). New York: Grune & Stratton, 1965.

8 Telephone Crisis Counseling

Crisis intervention by telephone has been the increasing focus of crisis and suicide-prevention centers around the world. While the focus of this book is upon in-person crisis counseling, many crisis clinics are extensively involved in telephone counseling and referral. Whether dealing with a person in crisis face to face or over the telephone, there are certain similarities in the approaches used.

Telephone intervention, while unique in many respects, nevertheless adheres closely to the principles of achieving contact with the person in crisis, boiling the problem down, assessing coping skills, and presenting a resolution plan. In addition, a telephone interview has as its components a beginning, middle, and ending phase. As in all interviews, there will be an interrelationship between these three stages and the principles described earlier in the book.

Beginning

This first stage of a crisis call begins the moment the telephone rings. The task is to establish contact and develop as much rapport as possible as early as possible without coming across as insincere and hurried. As with the face-to-face interview, the first few minutes are important. The manner in which the counselor handles this beginning stage may determine the course of events throughout the rest of the telephone interview. During this time, the counselor will be attempting to isolate crisis themes, assessing the caller's level of distress, and getting as much information about the situation as possible. In Chapter 5 we outlined a model designed to help in the organization of this material. While this outline is primarily designed for face-to-face counseling situations, it is also quite appropriate for telephone work as well, and we urge the reader to review it.

The beginning phase can be very stressful for the counselor. He cannot see his caller and therefore has only a mental picture. Because all the visual cues are missing, the nonverbal signals that can play a most helpful role in the counseling process are absent. Thus, the counselor is left to rely on the vocal and nonvocal sounds and situational content presented by the caller. Miller suggests that the counselor listen for voice inflections, background noises, and the like in order to reduce this handicap (1973).

As in all forms of crisis counseling, the counselor should offer only as much structure in the interview situation as the caller requires. If the caller is very talkative, the counselor should refrain from interfering too much. If the caller needs more support and direction, then the counselor should be prepared to offer it. As always, take your cues from the client and respond to *his* needs in determining how much or how little to guide the telephone interview.

Middle

This stage, as in face-to-face work, is the main body of the telephone counseling process. It is the period in which the counseling work is most clearly identified and the techniques outlined in Chapter 4 are applied. This stage develops as both the caller and the counselor are able to develop a mutual working relationship. It is in this stage that the counselor identifies the major features of the crisis state and the course of action he will pursue to find its ultimate solution.

The counselor will want to strike a balance between enabling the caller to talk about himself but not permitting him to ramble endlessly in his conversation. Middleton addresses herself to this point:

Allowing the caller to lead the conversation and helping him to feel that he can talk spontaneously are important, and yet the volunteer must usually provide some focus in the interview by questioning, paraphrasing, sharing his own feelings, making observations (1973).

As in all crisis work, the counselor must stay with the current situation as much as possible. He must avoid the trap of letting the caller spend most of the time talking about long-standing and chronic difficulties and get him to focus upon the immediate demands of his crisis. Whie this will require some tact and counseling skill, the client will benefit in the long run.

Telephone counseling is not particularly designed to take the place of long-term intensive psychotherapy involving detailed social and psychological history. It is focused in the "here and now," with the emphasis upon rapid resolution of the crisis situation. Frequently the counselor will have only a single opportunity to deal with the caller, thus he should not waste time in talking about chronic and often unresolvable situations.

In an attempt to clarify some aspects of this stage, Benjamin outlines several questions for the counselor to ask of himself:

1. Did you help the caller to look squarely at his own life situation and to explore and express it, or did he perceive himself through the eyes of someone else?
2. Did the caller discover his own self, or did he find a self he thought he should be finding?
3. Did you enable the caller to tell you how he genuinely feels and how things truly look to him?
4. Did you let the caller explore what he wanted to in his own way, or did you lead him in a direction you chose for him?
5. Did you help the caller to formulate and evaluate the range of options and choices open to him, limited as it may be? (1969)

Ending

This stage develops in the same fashion as does the ending phase of face-to-face counseling. The goals and processes are identical. It begins as the caller and counselor are mutually able to agree that all relevant issues and problems have been explored and identified. It involves summarization of what has been discussed to date. It is at this point that the intervention plan will be applied directly to the identified problems so as to bring relief from the distress that prompted the call. In addition, it is during this stage that it will be necessary to make an appropriate referral to whatever community resource will be likely to help the caller deal with those aspects of his situation that could not be handled on the phone. Again quoting Middleton: "Matching resources with the needs, taking into account variables such as finances, transportation, etc., and being aware of the caller's preferences all make the referral process much more than the mere giving of a phone number or address" (1973).

Having offered the referral, the counselor should recheck with the caller to make sure that he has the correct information, telephone number and address. Another important aspect of this phase is letting the caller know that you will make a follow-up call in the near future. During this follow-up, the counselor can see how the caller is doing, determine if he followed through with the referral, and review his current status.

Saying goodby on the telephone is sometimes easier than performing this in person. The same problems that are present in face-to-face termination are present in telephone work. They may not, however, be as intense. Nevertheless, the counselor will want to be quite sensitive in regard to this facet of the call and deal with it appropriately.

This brief summary of the essential principles of telephone counseling should in no way be construed as sufficient information to enable a counselor to consider himself qualified to serve immediately as a volunteer in a telephone-counseling service. For the most part, telephone-counseling services have an extensive inservice training program in which they require every volunteer to participate. The above information is just a beginning, designed to familiarize the prospective crisis counselor with some of the principles involved.

In summary, the telephone-counseling process has a structure similar to the face-to-face format. With experience, the telephone counselor will be able more easily to incorporate these concepts into a workable approach that will facilitate the process of effective crisis resolution. For a more in-depth analysis of telephone crisis intervention, the reader is directed to the work of Lester and Brockopp (1972).

References

Benjamin, A., ed. *Helping Interview*. Boston: Houghton Mifflin, 1969.
Lester, D., and G. Brockopp, eds. *Telephone Therapy and Crisis Intervention*. Springfield, Ill.: Charles Thomas, 1972.

Middleton, F. "The Interview Process." Mimeograph. Seattle: School of Social Work, University of Washington, 1973.

Miller, S. "Techniques of Telephone Intervention." Mimeograph. Seattle: School of Social Work, University of Washington, 1973.

Suggested Readings

Tabachnick, N., and Klugman, D.J. "No Name—A Study of Anonymous Suicidal Telephone Calls." *Psychiatry* 28 (1965): 79-87.

Crisis Intervention with Minority Group Clients

Thus far we have examined the concept of a crisis and the various techniques of crisis intervention without regard to the type of client. Perhaps it would be wise to briefly discuss crisis intervention in relation to one important client characteristic—race. Our discussion will focus mainly upon black clients, although some of the concepts are clearly applicable to other ethnic or racial minorities.

Inadequacies of Therapeutic Approaches with Black Clients

As a form of therapy, crisis intervention perhaps shares some of the criticisms leveled at psychotherapy and its responsiveness to black clients. Schofield has shown that most psychotherapists or mental health professionals prefer those client characteristics that would place most black clients at a disadvantage (1964). He found that therapists exhibited the "YAVIS" syndrome, preferring clients who were young, attractive, verbal, introspective, and successful. Obviously, many blacks (and other individuals, such as the poor) would not be considered "good" clients. Indeed, minority clients are often given less preferred forms of treatment (Yamamoto, James, and Palley 1968), perhaps because therapists avoid working with them directly.

But even when a black client enters into a therapeutic relationship with a white therapist, a number of difficulties often hinder the therapeutic process. The therapist as well as the client brings into the relationship attitudes and values that reflect the larger society. A white therapist who has not had a great deal of contact with minority groups may possess stereotypes and negative attitudes toward blacks. They, in turn, may feel suspicious and alienated toward white mental health workers. Since therapy requires some degree of trust, rapport, and a working relationship, black clients often find counseling or therapy useless and prematurely terminate. In an experimental study, Carkhuff and Pierce found that similarities between counselors and clients in race or social class facilitated a client's self-exploration, while differences in these characteristics hindered self-exploratory statements (1967).

The difficulties in black-white relations can be conceptualized at several different levels. First, as mentioned previously, there may be distrust, negative attitudes, and suspicion during the initial encounter, simply as a result of the general racial climate that the therapist and client have experienced. Second, the therapist may fail to understand the subculture of the minority client and thus neglect environmental limitations as well as environmental resources (strengths) that the client may have. Finally, traditional forms of psychotherapy may be inappropriately applied to the minority client. For example, attempts to adjust a client to a hostile environment may be unwise and fruitless when basic changes in the environment are necessary. To demand insight and personal changes in a client who lives in a destructive environment is inappropriate if environmental changes are more appropriate.

Crisis Intervention with Minority Clients

The basic goal of crisis intervention is to provide immediate, intensive, short-term help to clients in a state of crisis. Thus, many minority clients have been able to receive therapy without being placed on waiting lists or without being shuffled away to less preferred forms of treatment. In addition, many crisis services (hotlines, walk-in clinics) have been organized to help clients regardless of their financial resources. They have utilized minority-group counselors or therapists, encouraging a greater responsiveness to the needs of minority-group individuals in a state of crisis.

Obviously, to specify precisely how to conduct crisis therapy with minority-group individuals would ignore individual differences and be an exercise in racial stereotypes. There are, however, some critical issues that the counselor must examine.

In interacting with a crisis client, the counselor must accurately assess the nature and circumstances of the crisis. In doing so, the counselor should make special efforts to be aware of any biases and preconceptions that might influence his assessment of the minority-group client. Thomas and Sillen discuss the following errors that therapists often commit:

If he regards Black persons as "naturally" impulsive or emotional, he may decide that certain modes of behavior are not of psychiatric concern when they in fact reflect mental illness. Or he may commit the opposite error. If the clinician fails to take into account special environmental circumstances, he will misjudge normal behavior as pathological. He may label realistic anger as neurotic hostility (1972).

In order to minimize these errors, the counselor should, ideally, be sensitive to his own prejudices regarding minorities and know the minority client not only as an individual but also as a member of a disadvantaged group. It takes a very sensitive counselor to realize that minority clients do have experiences that differ from those of whites; however, not all of the client's problems need be attributed to race.

Another area that the counselor must attend to carefully is the subcultural values that the minority client maintains. This is important, since to strengthen the individual's resources in coping with a crisis, the counselor uses those resources available to the client. Subcultural values frequently help to determine the nature of resources. For example, suppose a Chinese-American client is experiencing a financial crisis; he has lost his job and has no means by which to support himself. The counselor may try to help this client by contacting a welfare agency without realizing that for the Chinese client to accept welfare would arouse a great deal of shame. Thus, the client is resistant to this alternative—one that would be acceptable to many other individuals—because of deeply rooted, culturally determined feelings of shame.

In conclusion, the counselor working with minority clients should be sensitive to prejudices and attitudes that can affect the assessment of the client's situation. He must also be sufficiently aware of the client's subcultural values and environment so that realistic coping strategies can be developed.

We do not believe that racial similarity between client and counselor is a necessary or sufficient condition for successful crisis intervention. However, when clients and counselors do differ in ethnic group membership, the counselors must be sensitive and aware if they are to facilitate rapport, respect, and a positive outcome.

References

Carkhuff, R.R., and R. Pierce. "Differential Effects of Therapist Race and Social Class Upon Patient Depth of Self-Exploration In the Initial Clinical Interview." *Journal of Consulting Psychology* 31 (1967): 632-34.

Schofield, W. *Psychotherapy: The Purchase of Friendship.* Englewood Cliffs, N.J.: Prentice-Hall, 1964.

Thomas, A., and S. Sillen. *Racism and Psychiatry.* New York: Brunner/Mazel, 1972.

Yamamoto, J., Q.C. James, and N. Palley. "Cultural Problems in Psychiatric Therapy." *Archives of General Psychiatry* 19 (1968): 45-49.

Part II
Case Histories

Introduction to Part II

The following section is designed to serve as a teaching and training instrument; it will not always be possible to deal with real-life situations in a similar fashion. In particular this refers to the use of the deductive model for analyzing each interview. In real life the counselor cannot divert so much of his attention from the client(s) to take such copious notes and identify each theme as it emerges. This would not only be impractical but quite inappropriate in the delivery of a crisis service. The counselor would lose contact with the client and spend much of his time writing and analyzing. In addition, the exacting detail with which the following cases are outlined would be quite cumbersome and awkward in a real situation. This section provides the reader with an opportunity to put into practice some of the principles and concepts that we have offered in the previous section.

In this section, case examples will be presented, representing a spectrum of situational crises that require counseling intervention. They are by no means the only kinds of cases that a counselor will be expected to deal with. They do, however, contain many of the elements typical of crisis situations. The case examples are selected from actual interviews. They have been edited to protect the identity of the clients, but the spirit of the crisis has been retained.

With each case we have provided the reader with an opportunity to put into practice what has been covered in the preceding chapters. A page has been provided for the reader to organize the interview material as if he were the counselor. Following that will be an explanation of how the interview should be organized and subsequently conducted. This format will be followed after each interview, thus giving the reader an opportunity to check himself.

In an ideal setting the interviews would be outlined with all of the appropriate interviewing and treatment concepts. As the reader will quickly see, however, this is not the case here. During the conduct of the crisis interviews the counselors made a certain number of errors. Thanks to the tape recorder and a strong tolerance for psychological stress by the closely supervised counselors, the mistakes of the interviews were later corrected and modified. The reader will have the benefit of experiencing some of the same mistakes, but without the consequences of doing it with real clients.

The format for handling all cases was as follows: The counselors would excuse themselves about five or ten minutes just prior to the end of the interview to discuss the case with the senior author. During this time precipitating events, the nature of the crisis, coping abilities, etc. were discussed. This process ordinarily took about five minutes. The counselor would then return to the interview and work out, with the client, the goals and homework for the next interview.

This format was both therapeutic as well as educational. In the first place it gave the clients an opportunity to assimilate some of the material that had been presented during the course of the interview. Frequently, they reported that while the counselor was gone they had had the opportunity to give more thought to what they had said and had come up with some additional insights.

For the counselor it was an opportunity to check out their perceptions of the crisis with their supervisor and receive immediate feedback. This break was also helpful when they were dealing with particularly disturbing cases that stressed the counselor's psychological resources to the limit. During this "breathing time" they could collect their thoughts and be in a better position to handle some of their feelings by sharing them with someone who was outside of the situation.

At no time did either the clients or the counselors consider this brief interruption detrimental to the counseling process. On the contrary, both parties commented positively about it and used the time to achieve a better grasp of the crisis dilemma. Certain precautions were taken with clients who were so upset that the absence of the counselor would have proven harmful. But these were the exceptional cases.

10 "No"

Jody, who was twenty-one and divorced, was seen four times over a six-week period. Her presenting problem was an inability to cope with family problems, particularly her younger sister. Divorced two years before, she feels restless inside now. She had attempted suicide one year before, but was not at that point now. She wanted to understand herself.

First Interview

Counselor: Do you want to tell me a little bit about what's been happening, Jody?

Client: I am just very restless inside and I'm at the point where it's hard for me to be around people. I feel like I just want to cry all the time and usually I can control my emotions, but as of late I go into fits of rage or I just don't want to be around anybody.

Counselor: As of late?

Client: About the last month it's been coming to a head.

Counselor: What happened a month ago?

Client: My sister took off. My folks were living in Wyoming. My sister's nineteen, she left home. And tracking her down and trying to find out where she was, and then the folks decided she had made the step herself and to leave her in Boise, and when I got a call from my sister-in-law about three weeks ago that she was in trouble, I took off work and went over there. She was living in a communal-type situation and what frightened her was one of the guys had gone freaky on a cocaine trip, and she was selling dope. My sister-in-law is here, but my sister had called her and told her that she wanted to come home. . . . My folks just don't want her home, so at that time she was going to live with me. I got a second job. A nighttime job so that if she wanted to go back to school I could help her.

Counselor: And you are living alone?

Client: No, I was living with my folks at the time because they had just come back from Wyoming, a job they were on. So then my sister left, and she's living around here with her boyfriend and another couple. It's just the tension. I'm in the middle between them and

101

my folks and what I feel I should do and what I do do, and what I'm allowed to do. It's just a rolling emotion that's been building up over a two-year period. For two years I haven't been able to settle down, or I'll get a job and start enjoying it or something, and then I'll quit or something. I can't get stable. . . . What I want to do right now is just get away from civilization. That's all I can think of. Just getting away from people. Getting away from my home. Getting away from my sister and my family and just letting them do their thing.

Counselor: So right now, as it stands, you're not happy where you are living. You would like to leave your parents' home.

Client: Yeah, I will be leaving shortly. . . . I'm planning on getting a small house out in the Greenwood area.

Counselor: Does that make you feel less anxious, that you will be moving out and moving into a home of your own?

Client: I really don't know. I get feelings like I would like to live with somebody my age, but being in the state of mind I am, I don't want anybody around. I don't want to have to put up with just the social talking or, like at work when I have a coffee break, I can't even stand to go in for coffee because I don't like the social chitchat. . . . I'm training girls under me and I'm getting so I have to fight to be pleasant. All I want to do is lunge at them and say get out of my life. . . . I just feel unstable.

Counselor: Can you give me some examples of what makes you feel unstable?

Client: I don't know what makes me that way. I'm flighty, like I'm never satisfied. One moment I can be in gay spirits and in an instant I can change to very depressed. I don't like this.

Counselor: What about your sleeping habits and all as of the last month?

Client: The last month, four nights a week I got three hours of sleep because I was working an extra job.

Counselor: Now you're not?

Client: No. I quit because I couldn't take the hours.

Counselor: So are the hours you are sleeping normal for you now?

Client: Yeah, to a point. Sometimes I can sleep all day and all night, and other times I can't sleep at all, or if I do it's a restless sleep. I wake up in a heavy sweat or just not be able to reach a sleep. (*Long pause.*)

Counselor: When you called in, you called because you were unable to cope with the family problem?

Client: No. They are going to have to settle that themselves. I realize that. But I'm getting worried about myself because, like Friday night I had a date. Now I don't usually go on dates, because I get too much of a hassle in my head because I don't like to play the games that guys play. I just like to go out and have a good time and that's it. Just leave it where it is. I had a date Friday night and he didn't show. I don't know for what reason. I was supposed to meet him for dinner. Now something like that's not something you would get upset about. I use my car a lot. I take it out and speed. I was crying so hard I couldn't see so I had to pull over to the side of the road. This kind of thing bothers me, because I can't control my emotions.

Counselor: It's understandable that if he didn't show up you might have——

Client: But this has never affected me before. Things just usually roll off my shoulder. I'm pretty easygoing. I get involved in other peoples' problems but to the point of where if I feel I can't do anything, I just leave it lay where it is. But now, I can't let things roll off.

Counselor: How do your parents feel about your living alone and moving out of their house?

Client: They don't care one way or the other. If I live there, fine; if I move, fine. We have a strong family pride, and if one were to get in trouble, the whole family rallies to support. But as far as a warm family relationship, sitting down and talking and laughing, that's almost void in our home. We have never been together like a family. Everybody has got their separate directions to go. . . . My father is a very quiet man. He doesn't talk. He does a lot of looks. His looks can cut you in half. He can give you a look that can make you wish you could die at the moment. But he doesn't usually say very much. . . . His approach or his eye contact is enough to warn you off. And my mother, she never shuts up. (*Laughing.*) She's one of these neurotic people you can take for half an hour. . . .

Counselor: So then what you really would like to talk about here is your being able to control your reactions.

Client: Yes. This is what I'm beginning to worry about. . . . This has really got me in a frenzy.

Counselor: Well, I understand. I hear what you say about that. Is there anything else that you would like to work on, or hope to resolve?

Client: I don't know. Like today when I was sitting there, I'd think after I had made the appointment, well, gee, you can handle it yourself. Why go and talk to somebody? When I was in Boise and I'd get scared for no reason. You know, everything was going good. But I'd get inwardly frightened and I had made a call to a minister. At that time I was in the Lutheran faith and I hadn't been in contact with anybody, so I called to talk to somebody why I would get these feelings. But when I called, they said, sorry you had to make an appointment. Well, what's the point? I can handle it myself. . . . It started about two years ago after my divorce. Out of the blue I can just be sitting and I've got a fear, or—I don't know how to explain the feeling. If I don't get away, then I'm trapped in a situation, though there may be no situation. I just want to take off. Something will happen. Don't ask me what, because I have no idea. But I just get upset and afraid of things that don't exist. . . .

Counselor: What about the circumstances around your divorce? What about what was happening at the time you actually broke up?

Client: I think about it a lot, but I don't really understand. I think there was a lot of immaturity on my part. My husband, when I first met him, was a fantastic, gentle man, but he got involved with dope . . . and this brought me into contact with people I couldn't cope with because in our family you just take No-Doze. . . . After a while I just couldn't cope with it, so I left.

Counselor: How did your husband feel about it?

Client: He was upset at first, but then he thought it would be better too. We tried talking about getting back together, but by that time his mother had been too far involved, and she was a very domineering person, and she started working on him. We couldn't reach out and get back. We couldn't find a meeting point. Perhaps if his mother had been out of the picture, maybe we could have gotten back together.

Counselor: Would you want that?

Client: (*Crying.*) I don't know what I want. I think about it a lot. I've tried locating him, but there would be really no point in that, because things being the way they are, I just don't think we could do it. So I just let it pass on. There's not much I can do about it. . . . (*Long pause.*)

Counselor: There is some information I didn't get earlier that I'm kind of concerned about, and that is you say you're afraid of what you will do?

Client: It's not to the point of what I will do, like suicide or anything, but I get so outrageously upset.

Counselor: About the suicide. What about any thoughts of suicide or plans?

Client: No. Sometimes you think about it. You say what really is the point of living, because everybody is playing their little games and there is just nothing to tie down to. What is the rock or foundation you can go from? You just seem to be wandering with no purpose, no goal, nothing. You think, wouldn't it be nice just to lay down and just forget about the whole world? But you can't because there are so many beautiful things around.

Counselor: So this is not a plan of yours—suicide?

Client: No, never.

Counselor: But it has been in the past?

Client:	(*Voice shaky.*) Yes, I had a suicidal attempt when I was in Boise.
Counselor:	What exactly did you do?
Client:	I overdosed.
Counselor:	Were you alone?
Client:	At the time, yes, I was. I was living with a woman and two children.
Counselor:	You were alone in the home, and you overdosed on what?
Client:	It was just Bufferin, Anacin, and aspirin.
Counselor:	What happened?
Client:	They took me to the hospital and pumped my stomach and sent me home. There were a couple of cops that came on the scene and got smart and I got smart back with them, and they didn't like that too well.
Counselor:	You did overdose, and you were alone in the house, but somebody undoubtedly found you.
Client:	The woman came home, and she and her date took me.
Counselor:	And how did you feel afterward about that?
Client:	Very much alone.
Counselor:	Did you see anybody after your return home, any kind of counselor, any kind of followup?
Client:	No. I had no counseling on that. It was just an aspect of life I had touched, didn't really care for, and dropped it.
Counselor:	This isn't a thought with you now?
Client:	No.
Counselor:	How long has it been since the suicide attempt?
Client:	Last summer.
Counselor:	So it has been a year ago?
Client:	Uh huh. . . .

At this point the counselor excuses herself from the interview with the explanation that she wants to consult with her supervisor. Keep in mind that the themes will always be influenced by the counselor's biases, the attitude of the client, the intensity of the crisis moment, and the school of thought and theoretical background that the counselor's supervisor follows.

DEDUCTIVE MODEL

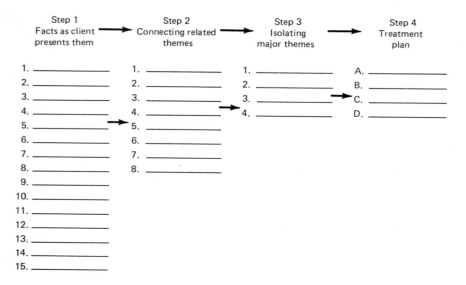

| Step 1
Facts as client
presents them | Step 2
Connecting related
themes | Step 3
Isolating
major themes | Step 4
Treatment
plan |

1. _____ 1. _____ 1. _____ A. _____
2. _____ 2. _____ 2. _____ B. _____
3. _____ 3. _____ 3. _____ C. _____
4. _____ 4. _____ 4. _____ D. _____
5. _____ 5. _____
6. _____ 6. _____
7. _____ 7. _____
8. _____ 8. _____
9. _____
10. _____
11. _____
12. _____
13. _____
14. _____
15. _____

Additional comments:

Step 1 Facts as Client Presents Them	*Step 2* Connecting Related Themes	*Step 3* Isolating Major Themes	*Step 4* Treatment Plan

restless inside
want to cry
fits of rage
away from people
1 month ago
sister ran
drugs
now living with cl.
helping her
in the middle
between family
began 2 yrs. ago
can't get stable
want to run
stood up
real upset
car speeding
can't control emotions
other people's problems
afraid of dad
major worry/control
  emotions
unexplained fears
ambiv. about help
divorce two yrs. ago
second job
	1 month ago
	–sis. trouble
	–family stress
	–second job
	–stood up
	
	Unable to cope
	–friends' probs.
	–wants to run
	–work pressures
	–can't control emotions
	
	Feels
	–depressed
	–fits of rage
	–crying
	–trapped
	–restless inside
	–afraid
	–unexplained fears
	
	Strengths
	–identify stress points
	–prev. success crisis
	  history
	–reasoning ability
	–motivation
	–routines
		Crisis situation
		–events
		–verbal report
		–behavior
		
		Coping skills
		–not danger to self/others
		
		Connected themes
		–can't set limits
		–unable to assert
		–can't control emotions
		
		Danger to self/others
		–not severe
			Tell her she is in crisis
			
			Allow to ventilate
			  (Focus on prec. events)
			Help control emotions
			  (self management)
			
			Consider assertive training
			
			Gather more information

Additional Comments:

Second Interview—Summary

During this session, Jody reported lessening of some pressures but still felt unable to say no to the demands of some of her friends and family. "I try to sit down and logically reason with them, but after awhile they just close in on me and I feel like I'm selfish. . . . I feel guilty."

About her feelings of nervousness around people: "It's toning down. When I first came in here I didn't want to be around anybody at all . . . now . . . I'm more relaxed. I mean, I can do my job and keep my mind on that."

She reported that her feelings of loneliness were still with her, and on reflection saw this as a chronic problem. "I don't attach to people that much. I stay aloof in a lot of respects." She saw this as a result of many geographical moves. "There was no time to attach. There was no real foundation. You just get to meet people and have to say goodby to them. . . . It just seems like past sixth grade there seems to be a void." In high school, "I graduated with kids I didn't even know. My big graduation night was nothing. It's just been that way. There is just nothing to hold on to." During high school she excelled in gymnastics and other athletic events.

In response to a question about her ability to control some of her emotions, she said, "My control is getting better. I'm busy and I'm not snapping . . . like I was." However, "Panic moments I still can't control . . . and . . . I can't figure out why." When she has these restless and panicky feelings, she says, "I just have to get away . . . getting in my car and driving. Turning on the radio. Just getting out and going. Clearing my head. Going to the beach or just running."

She was unable to more clearly define her feelings of "restlessness." "I can't put it into words." She described her growing up: "My life style was set for me and I never went against my parents. I never went against my father. Whatever was said was law. I never skipped school, nothing. I wasn't a rebellious kid or anything. I was perfect in school."

The status of her sister remains the same. She is still living with her boyfriend. And Jody spent almost no time talking about her.

Due to the summary of this interview, we present the completed diagram rather than having the reader outline it.

Second Interview

1. Current Status of Client's Crisis

First Interview	This Interview
restless inside	little change
people making demands	no change
being around people	some change/at work, no much/at home
loneliness/talking	no change/can talk with coun.
self-control	better
ident. restlessness	little or no success
living arrangements	about same
precip. event/sister	same/still living with friends

2. Current Status of Crisis Intervention Plan

First Interview	This Interview
tell her she's in crisis and "normalize" behavior	doesn't feel so estranged and "flipped"
allow to talk	prob. most effective
help control emotions	not completely clear
consider assertive training	yes, have her start this week

3. New Information
   a. chronic history of loneliness and how she attempted to cope
   b. more family and social history
   c. consequences of previous assertive attempts
   d. new events; nothing significant

4. Crisis Intervention Plan for Next Session
   a. Introduce Assertive Training and explain
   b. Keep an eye on negative consequences of being assertive, go slow
   c. Reinforce attempts and previous areas of successful problem solving, e.g. athletics, using her head (thinking)

Third Interview

Counselor: What's been happening?

Client: Well, Saturday my sister moved out of her boyfriend's place, so she is living with my brother and his wife. Their baby is supposed to begin X-ray Thursday for something like a kidney disorder or something. So it's kind of tough right now. Everybody is in a real heavy, depressed mood over things, and so I'm supposed to go out and get an apartment so my sister can live with me, which I don't really mind, but there are so many things to worry about and think about.

Counselor: Like what?

Client: Like her age and her friends. I don't like a lot of her friends. I wouldn't want them hanging around all the time. . . . She's only seventeen now, and there is a difference in our age and what we like, and it just seems like it might be a rough go. Plus the fact, on $300 a month it's rough supporting myself, let alone her. . . . Finding a place I could afford is a little bit hairy close enough to where Mickie could get work if she tried. Her attitude frightens me. I don't know if she is going to up and take off or what she's going to do. She's got a handicap anyway. She has not graduated. She has no diploma, so there are only a few types of jobs open to her, and I try to explain to her that she cannot apply for a job barefoot and in blue jeans. It just doesn't go into her head. . . . And then there is Jean. Five minutes after I get home Jean is calling me and wants me to come down and give her a rubdown, or come down and sit and listen to her. It's just beginning to get to me.

Counselor: How are you handling that, Jody, when someone calls you like Jean and asks you to do something you don't want to do?

Client: I think about it, you know. I think, well, she's got problems and it doesn't hurt for somebody to listen, but she's smothering me. I finally had to ask her to quit calling me at work. She was calling me two or three times a day.

Counselor: And you did ask her to stop calling?

Client: Yeah, I can't afford to lose my job with the situation the way it is. Otherwise I'd just throw my hands up, let them take my car, and I'd take off. It's just a momentary thing, but it's at the point where nowhere you turn can you get out of it, and there is nothing you can do. Everybody has decided my life for me from the time I get home. I tried to read for a little while last night. Mother wants me to run to the store, Candy wants me to baby-sit, Jean wants me to bring her some apple juice because her baby is sick and she can't get out, and it's just everybody has got my life planned. There is just no time.

Counselor: So you go along with what requests they make of you?

Client: It's too much of a hassle to stand up. . . . I told my mother the other day I was flat out not going up to that hospital to see the baby. For one thing, I don't like hospitals, and for another, I just couldn't stand the idea of seeing that baby and knowing the condition it might be in, and then having something happen to it. I'd rather just divorce myself from the thing and when the baby comes home in fine health, fine, then I will be there.

Counselor: Getting back to what you said a minute ago. I think you said it's too much of a hassle to stand up and say no.

Client: It is. It really is. . . . Like, if Candy or Dave ask me to baby-sit and I said No, then they get uptight about it. . . . It makes me feel like a slob. It makes me feel really selfish. They are right. My brother is in a situation and he can use my services and why aren't I more enthused about helping out? I get a shamed feeling. They do a job on my head, and boy they can really do it.

Counselor: What do you think you can do to control their requests?

Client: Move out and get away from them. They are controlling it now because I am living there at home and every night I ask if I can help with the dinner or dishes or something I can do for Mom, and no there is nothing I can do. Then like last night, Candy wanted Mom to baby-sit and she wasn't feeling up to it, so Dad just really got up tight and said, "Well, why don't you do it?" I said, "Well, yeah, I can." All I wanted to do last night is take a bath and read.

Counselor: How about if you said that?

Client: (*Laughing.*) "No."

Counselor: What would happen?

Client: There would be a lot of tension in the house. Because first of all, you just don't talk to my dad that way, and second of all, you're supposed to pitch in and help when they need it, whether you want to or not. It's an obligation of blood. . . . My dad really knows how to cut you down to nothing without saying a word. His actions, his looks. He's very good at cutting me down with a look. Ever since I was little he has been able to do that to me. . . . He just has a way about him that makes you feel ashamed. I don't know what to be ashamed of, but he has a way of making you feel ashamed. When I was in high school and I was dating, it seemed like every guy I went out with, my mother would give me a lecture for two hours on sex before they got there. Then my dad had done his little . . . thing. He was always afraid I was going to whip out and lay everybody I could. I never did anything wrong. I never even skipped school. I was a perfect B student, and anything they wanted, I never questioned. . . . I wish one of these times I could just flat out and say, "Blah," and he'd probably knock me on my tail. (*Laughing.*)

Counselor: What about the demands other people make on you? Your friends. How can you control that?

Client: I don't know. The only one I'm having problems with is Jean, and she is suffocating me. She expects me to come over every night and have a drink with her and talk with her on the phone all day—and you know, you just——

Counselor: And you don't want to?

Client: No. I don't mind talking to her and that, but it gets a little bit on your nerves if it's all the time. She's in an emotional state and I can't handle hers and mine too, and my family's. . . .

Counselor: Is it difficult for you to say no to your girlfriends?

Client: Yes, it really is. Because she gets upset and that, and she wants somebody to talk to and you just don't want to, but if you say no, then you're afraid of what she might interpret it as. If you think about it a little longer, then you think, "I can remember when there was nobody to talk to," so why not . . . and I don't have the nerve to flat out and say no, I want to do something for me.

Counselor: How about developing that nerve?

Client: Yeah. How do you do it without getting the guilty feelings of being so selfish?

Counselor: Well, you could try it with your friend. . . . Between now and next week, you could try it in a nice way. Explain how you feel, and what's going on with you right now. You want some time to be alone. You want some time to take a bath, do your own hair, or whatever. . . . See what the outcome is. I'd be interested to hear how you feel when you carry through.

Client: I don't know. It's just trying to do it.

Counselor: Could you try it once?

Client: (*Pause.*) Yeah.

Counselor: I was listening to the tape, Jody, and you mentioned something about doing gymnastics in school, being pretty good at it. I wonder, do you have any outlet like that now?

Client: No.

Counselor: What about developing some interest in a mountaineer club that does hiking?

Client: I never thought about it other than like running or something. I just never have. I've thought about going to the Y and getting into gymnastics again, and I go swimming . . . but I can't take my scuba lessons until I get my teeth fixed, which they just told me is going to cost the price of a VW, so I'm checking into getting dentures.

Counselor: Well, in the meantime maybe you could check into the gymnastics at the Y. That couldn't be too terribly expensive (*Pause.*) So now what about the decision to move out of your mother and father's home and into an apartment with your sister?

Client: I don't like the idea, because I know it's going to be financially bad. An apartment is going to run at least $100 a month, and I've got about $150 a month going out in bills, and I only make $300. I thought about going down and talking to Welfare and see about getting food stamps or something that could help us out until she gets a job. She wants to go out and get a real nice apartment. . . . If I just said no and moved out of my family's home and set up for my ownself, taking care of myself, it would be looked upon as a very selfish child.

Counselor: And how would that make you feel?

Client: Like a slob. My divorce separated my father, and my family, and I for a while, and I didn't like it. I'm just getting back on the grounds now, until this baby situation came up. It seems like all my life I try so hard to please my father and nothing seems to work. Mom says he's happy with the way we kids do, but he never shows any expression of it. But that's neither here nor there. But I will be getting an apartment this week, and what comes, comes. I can handle it, because I've always handled whatever has happened. But it's frightening, to say the least.

Counselor: So you're going to move out into an apartment regardless, whether with your sister or by yourself?

Client: I'm going to take Friday as vacation. I have some dental appointments, and I decided I was going to find a place. That's all there is to it. I feel like I'm a hindrance to my folks right now, although I enjoy having somebody around when I come home. I don't particularly care if I live by myself all the time. . . . If I had my way, I'd just move out of this area. If I had a job somewhere else I'd split in two minutes. I really would. I should have stayed in Boise. You get over here with the family mess-ups and everything, and they just turn you upside down. It's just too confusing. I can't keep up with them.

Counselor: But you want to be able to assert yourself.

Client: Yeah, and I'll have that opportunity when I move out, more so than I do now, because I can get away from them. It's not that I don't love my family, it's just (*pause*), I don't know . . . I just don't have the courage or whatever it takes to tell people I'm going to do what I want to do, because then I feel I'm being very selfish.

Counselor: But could you continue to try to develop that?

Client: Yeah. I don't have much confidence when I'm around my family. When I was in Boise I took care of myself okay. I had several things come up I had to handle, and I did it okay. But when I get here, boy they can turn me inside out. I don't know whether I'm up or down, or what.

Counselor: When the situation comes up, maybe developing that assertiveness, standing up and saying it, would be a help to you.

Client: It probably would. Maybe I just need to learn how to do it. I've just done it this way so long I just accept it.

Counselor: Jody, I want you to take it step by step. Assert yourself to Jean. Say, "No, tonight I want a shower or I'm going to do my own hair and this is why." On the big things, don't feel pushed to have to make a snap decision. Do what you feel comfortable with. Step a little slowly becoming more assertive with the little things, then more assertive with something that's more important to you, and eventually being able to stand up for what you really feel. Okay?

The counselor steps outside the office to consult about the case.

THIRD INTERVIEW

1. Current Status of Client's Crisis

Previous Interview	This Interview

2. Current Status of Crisis Intervention Plan

Previous Interview	This Interview

3. New Information

    a.

    b.

    c.

4. Crisis Intervention Plan for Next Session

    a.

    b.

THIRD INTERVIEW

1. Current Status of Client's Crisis

Previous Interview	This Interview
restless	better, still not identified
demands from others	same but handling better
living arrangements	making plans to move
sister	same
self control	better
loneliness	doesn't say much about it
assertiveness introd.	some small success, a first step

2. Current Status of Crisis Intervention Plan

Previous Interviews	This Interview
began assertiveness training	some success, has negative conseq. when with family, better with friend, not sure about sister
allow to talk	still fine

3. New Information
   a. Athletic history and activities, formerly a way to reduce tension

4. Crisis Intervention Plan for Next Session
   a. Continue assertiveness training on step-by-step basis
   b. Try athletics or other recreational activities
   c. Continue to reinforce strengths and coping abilities

Fourth Interview

Counselor: So it's been a couple of weeks. Shall we just start out with what's happening?

Client: Things are getting on an even keel.

Counselor: I'm glad to hear that.

Client: I've been very relaxed and very happy the last couple of weeks.

Counselor: You look different. You look good.

Client: (*Laughing.*) I spent a weekend over at Lake Eleanor taking care of four children over the long holiday and I water skiied and I laid in the sun. The kids were just fantastic, and I've been meeting kids over there my own age, and it's been a real outlet. I joined the women's softball team.

Counselor: Oh, good.

Client: I'm a little bit sore. . . . I've been trying to stay away pretty much from the family problems. Like the other night, my mother got on the topic of Mickie, and I just told her I didn't want to talk about it because I didn't think it was worth the fighting about if we couldn't sit down and talk about it. Mickie is waiting for two jobs. She might get a job at a cleaners or a live-in baby sitter, which I think would help her quite a bit, if she gets away from the family. I'm moving out the first of the month.

Counselor: Did you assert yourself to your friend?

Client: No.

Counselor: You didn't? (*Surprised.*)

Client: Not then I didn't. She called me the other day and she said would I like to come over, and I said "No, thank you. I have other things to do," which was true. I didn't have to lie about it or anything. But it seems that the last two weeks have been concentrated on me. . . . I frosted my hair. I was just getting tired of looking like a drab. I wanted something. They say it doesn't do much, but it does pick you up a little bit . . . and I've been dating this one guy. He's a planner for Glenn County. He's a very quiet man, but he is very stern. I think I need that, because he is the opposite of me. Like, he doesn't get involved in everybody's problems. He can think and see things more logically than I can, so he has a tendency to shut me down on some of these things, which I think is good.

Counselor: When you're talking about them to him, he'll say . . . ?

Client: Like with my sister, he says that (*laugh*) she's taking the easy way out and my folks have the right to feel the way they do, and if she really wanted to straighten out, she would go back to school. . . . He's very firm in his convictions. I believe he has a tencency to be soft, but he's very strict. He demands certain things be done certain

ways, which is pretty good. I think I need that in a relationship. . . . But I have been very selfish in the last two weeks.

Counselor: And it feels good?

Client: Yes, I feel very good. I feel very happy. I don't know how to explain it. It's hard to believe I can feel so relaxed as I do now.

Counselor: What do you think about moving out?

Client: Scared.

Counselor: Why?

Client: I don't know. It's just like walking again. You have to do it, and once you take the initial step it's all right, but you've got to get to it. You've got to get to the first step, and that's the scary part.

Counselor: So you feel scared, but do you feel anything else?

Client: Confident.

Counselor: Do you find that the more you practice asserting yourself, the easier it becomes?

Client: Yeah. Just like last Thursday, my sister was in my car when I got off work and she had been kicked out of my brother's home. So I took her straight back to Candy and Dave's. We sat down and just got it all out in the open, because I told them I'm not going to put up with it anymore. I have just had it. We were either going to get it straightened out or they can expect me to bow out, because I'm not going to do it anymore. I told Mickie, if she doesn't get a job, that's fine. She's going to make it so that nobody is going to want to respond to help her.

Counselor: Now when you said, "If it doesn't get squared away I'm going to bow out," how did they accept that?

Client: Mickie started looking for a job and she's got a job. A live-in baby sitter.

Counselor: Does she listen to you?

Client: Get out there and growl at them a little bit. It's a strange feeling. All of a sudden I'm a tiger—don't cross me. . . . There have been tight moments, but it's not like it was before. I'm not as keyed up and tied up as I was before.

Counselor: How about how often you are feeling this lost feeling we talked about before?

Client: I haven't had time for it.

Counselor: Do you remember feeling it at all in the last couple of weeks?

Client: Oh, maybe in quiet moments. Like, I walk over to the beach sometimes just for the peace, but it's an appreciated quietness.

Counselor: Your thoughts are different when you are alone?

Client: Uh, huh.

Counselor: Tell me about them.

Client: Oh, it's just like sitting and daydreaming and everything smells so clear over the beach and listening to the water. Just sitting there doing nothing.

Counselor: It's pleasant to you?

Client: Uh huh.

Counselor: That's such a change, Jody, from the first time you told me how you felt when you were alone and your heart would pound. Do you remember?

Client: Yes, I remember. . . . It started that weekend I spent over at the lake. . . . I spent some time getting to know the people over there. They are very nice young people. Party a lot. Ski, sports, very athletically inclined. I just haven't had time to sit down and be upset. I started the softball game and my father gets so irritated with me. He says I'm just too independent of men.

Counselor: Why did he say that?

Client: Because I don't date that much. I haven't been dating that much. If I go out with a man and he makes a wrong move toward me or, you know, I just prefer not to date him again. My dad just doesn't understand, but I don't have to take a lot of things that are dished out. You don't have to take anything you don't want to.

Counselor: No, you don't.

Client: Like last Friday night, Mom and Dad were going out to dinner, and all I wanted to do was do my hair and my dad says, "If you weren't so damn independent, you'd be going out tonight," and I said, "But I don't want to." Then he says, "Oooow."

Counselor: Then how did you feel about that? After confronting him?

Client: It was kind of comical. It didn't bother me a bit. (*Laughing.*) Maybe it's perhaps because I've been dating this one man. I don't know what the change is.

Counselor: How long have you been dating him?

Client: For a week. It started, well, the weekend of the long holiday, and it's just been very pleasant since. I've laid on the beach, stayed away from my family, and just had a ball.

Counselor: Is it easy to talk to this fellow?

Client: Yes. He's very quiet. I was over at his house Monday evening, and he had written a thesis on a population type thing, and he was talking to his professor on the phone and got very uptight, but not verbally. He hung up and went over to some friends for dinner and when we came back, he was in a mood. You know, he was just all bent up inside. So we had a few words and I thought, well, this is it. But doggone if he didn't call me back.

Counselor: So in other words, you spoke your mind to him and brought it out in the open that he was acting kind of like a——

Client: Little kid.

Counselor:	And you called him on it, and he accepted it?
Client:	Uh huh. He was mad when I left though and I said, "Gee, I didn't expect you to call or talk to me again." He says, "What for?" and I said, "Well we did have a difference of opinion last night." He says, "Well that was yesterday." (*Laughing.*)
Counselor:	Good.
Client:	He's very quiet and it's hard for me to get used to, because it's an uncomfortable quiet until—like we'll be together for ten or fifteen minutes and he won't say anything. Then you start talking and it's fascinating to listen to him talk, and I enjoy it.
Counselor:	Now where are you moving?
Client:	Probably out to the Lake Eleanor area. I like the people out there. There are a lot of young people that are single living out there—girls and guys—and everybody seems to have so much fun. You do your eight-hour thing at work, then come home, and the rest of it's playtime.
Counselor:	So it sounds like you're looking forward to moving?
Client:	Yes. I'm excited about it. I think it will be really quite fun. Everybody is skiing. Everybody has a boat or a bike. I'd like to get a bike this summer.
Counselor:	So that's where it is right now. What about all the problems we talked about when you first came in, remember?
Client:	I don't know. It seems that everything has been going so smooth. It's quite a different turnabout from what I felt when I first came in here.
Counselor:	Good. Would you say you are back to functioning the way you were before it all came about?
Client:	I think a little bit better. . . .
Counselor:	Well then, Jody, what do you feel about coming back anymore?
Client:	I've been thinking about it and I don't know. Things seem to be going pretty smooth right now, I don't feel as uptight about things as I did when I first came in here. Everything is in the past. There are going to be trying moments, I know that, but (*pause*) it's just, I feel contented inside.
Counselor:	And you feel you could cope if there was a loss or if something went wrong?
Client:	Yeah. I feel I could handle just about anything. I'm not saying by myself, but I'd make a darn good try at it. I've been away from Jean quite a bit the last two weeks. I've tried to stay away from her and her problems as much as I can. In fact, I just told the world to go blow.

The counselor steps out of the office to consult.

120

FOURTH INTERVIEW

1. Current Status of Client's Crisis

Previous Interviews	This Interview

2. Current Status of Crisis Intervention Plan

Previous Interviews	This Interview

3. New Information
   a.
   b.

4. Crisis Intervention Plan for Remainder of Session
   a.
   b.
   c.
   d.
   e.

Fourth Interview

1. Current Status of Client's Crisis

Previous Interviews	This Interview
family problems	staying away from same, setting limits on others
demands from others	still coming but saying no with some success, few negat. conseq.
loneliness	met new people, tentative boyfriend
restlessness	still not defined but more relaxed
moving	solid plans but scared
sister	still a problem but temp. relieved
controlling emotions	much improved
divorce material	unclear if settled or not

2. Current Status of Crisis Intervention Plan

Previous Interviews	This Interview
assertiveness	making a good beginning with several successes
self-management	improving
normalize crisis react.	not clear if this accomplished, didn't check it out
encouraged to talk	continued to be successful
reinforce coping skills	though not always made clear to client, she probably picked it up

3. New Information
   a. Client and counselor agree to terminate as crisis appears to be pretty well resolved.

4. Crisis Intervention Plan for Remainder of Session
   a. Reinforce client's success at handling many of the stressful events that brought her in. Do this by pointing out in 1, 2, 3 fashion where she was when she came in and where she is now.
   b. Emphasize an awareness of what client did that helped her regain self-control and self-management.
   c. Remind client that problems will not disappear but that her ability to solve them has improved.
   d. Ask if a referral for longer-term counseling would be in order. The focus could be upon:
      identifying and mastering "restlessness"
      chronic family problems and feeling trapped
      fear of men
      strengthen assertiveness skills
   e. Spend time in saying goodby. Verbalize it and give both client and counselor time to complete this process. A handshake or some other formalized way of saying goodby should be considered.

Discussion

During the actual intervention process, the counselor isolated most of what we considered to be the major crisis themes. However, in reexamining the case on the tapes, it became clear that she underemphasized and we overlooked several important facts.

To begin with, Jody's tension and agitation in the first two interviews should have been dealt with more directly. The counselor might have had Jody begin a homework assignment of trying to identify objectively the "restless feelings," what they were, when they began, how long they lasted, what cues may have set them off, etc.

This behavioral diary should have been kept during the duration of the counseling sessions. Whether this anxiety could ever be resolved within the crisis model or not is questionable. However, at the very least, Jody could have been helped in taking direct action towards more clearly describing the feelings she wanted to deal with.

In addition, a relaxation training program to deal with her agitation might have been initiated. Though relaxation alone would not have been sufficient, its use in combination with the other techniques would have been more appropriate.

In analyzing the outcome of this case, there may be some who would consider the successful resolution not to be really as good as it seems, but rather a case of the "hello-goodby" effect. This is where the client senses the counselor's emotional involvement in his improvement to be so great that he doesn't want to disappoint the counselor by failing to report progress. This may have been a component of the case. However, there was considerable behavioral evidence that Jody was engaging in a number of observable, positive changes: a trip to the lake, new boyfriend, athletics, etc. A six-month follow-up confirmed the validity of these changes. Jody reported that she had her own apartment, was still active athletically, still dating, and that she felt she was coping with stresses pretty well.

Let us next look briefly at some of the technical errors the counselor made during the conduct of the case:

1. In the first interview the counselor should have explored in more detail the previous suicide attempt. Unanswered are the questions: Why now? What triggered the action? What were the circumstances surrounding the attempt? What was the amount she took? What, if any, signals did she offer, indicating how upset she was? Was she really sent home immediately? Any time there is a previous suicide attempt, the counselor will want to ask about the five *w*'s: who? what? when? where? and why now?

2. We are of the opinion that persons in crisis need to know that many of their behavioral and feeling responses are "normal" given the circumstances of their situation. This "normalization" approach often relieves the client from

feeling that he is "going crazy" and helps him see his situation in slightly more realistic terms. The counselor had several opportunities to do this but was not as direct as she should have been.

3. Lastly, the counselor should have spent more time working with the divorce material. There appeared to be considerable feelings associated with the event as evidenced by the fact of Jody's crying, her attempts to locate him, and her feeling that the mother-in-law was the major obstacle to their reconciliation. In addition, Jody identified the divorce as precipitating some of her internal distress. Whether this was accurate or not was never explored or dealt with.

Suggested Readings

Agel, J. *The Radical Therapist.* New York: Ballantine Books, 1971.

Alberti, R.E., and M.L. Emmons. *Your Perfect Right: A Guide to Assertive Behavior.* San Luis Obisco, Cal.: Impact Books, 1970.

Cameron, N.A. *Personality Development and Psychopathology: A Dynamic Approach.* Boston: Houghton Mifflin, 1963.

Darwin, C. *The Expression of the Emotions in Man and Animals.* New York: Philosophical Library, 1955.

Ellis, A., and R.A. Harper. *A Guide to Rational Living.* Beverly Hills, Cal.: Wilshire Books, 1961.

Franks, V., and V. Burtle. *Women in Therapy: New Psychotherapies for a Changing Society.* New York: Brunner/Mazel, 1974.

Goldfried, M.R., and M. Merbaum, eds. *Behavior Change through Self-Control.* New York: Holt, Rinehart and Winston, 1973.

Haley, J. *Strategies of Psychotherapy.* New York: Grune & Stratton, 1963.

Lazarus, A.A. *Behavior Therapy and Beyond.* New York: McGraw-Hill, 1971.

Rogers, C.R., and B. Stevens. *Person to Person: The Problem of Being Human.* Lafayette, Cal.: Real Press, 1973.

Watson, D.L., and R.G. Tharp. *Self-Directed Behavior: Self-Modification for Personal Adjustment.* Monterey, Cal.: Brooks/Cole, 1972.

11 "Tell Me What To Do"

The client described in the following pages is a twenty-four-year-old woman who is separated and lives outside the hospital's service catchment area. During the course of the single interview in which Sandy was seen, she presented problems involving drug use and depression. Two psychiatrists had advised her to seek an evaluation of her condition at the hospital. The client reported having taken some "reds" (barbiturates) within the twenty-four hours prior to the interview.

Throughout the interview, which was conducted in the emergency room of a community hospital, the client's voice was flat, unemotional, and monotonous with little inflection. Her speech was slurred at times and there was frequent sniffling. She sat hunched over in the chair and rarely looked up from the floor.

Counselor: Tell me what's been going on.

Client: I don't know where to start. I started taking drugs when I was about sixteen. Before that I tried to commit suicide when I first started my sophomore year of high school. I was in the University Hospital in a mental ward for a while with Dr. Salzman, and he said I should get away and change my environment. I went to California and started smoking weed. Then I came back, and I really didn't do a lot of it, but still, I almost had a thought like when I'd get down, like there wasn't any sense of living. It was just so bad that it would be better if I just wasn't living at all.

I came back here and started school again but then dropped out after my junior year, was three months pregnant, got married, and when the baby was three months old I separated, and went back to him and got pregnant again. Then I left him when I was three months pregnant. I have a boy and a girl now. I didn't take drugs or smoke pot or anything for a long time, all the time I was pregnant with my second child. . . .

My husband had gotten strung out. He's addicted to heroin now. He had gotten strung out while we were separated. He'd try all kinds of stuff. Then I didn't start hitting up until last winter and it was the first time I had ever used morphine, and I've just been hitting up off and on since then. I've quit, but really I haven't ever quit taking drugs. I've quit for a couple months, but then I'd always go back. I've been busted and I'm on probation now.

I've tried hard to change the environment but it seems like

125

anymore around here or where I live, everywhere, there is no end to it. There are drugs everywhere no matter how hard you try to get away from them, they are there. Especially in this area. In the past four or five years it's just really bad. I've watched a lot of friends of mine who are as addicted as I am, and I don't know, it's a hard thing to face. I always say I'm not strung out, but yet I've never really stopped long enough to know. I couldn't really say I was strung out, but it depresses me and makes the problems I had then, a long time ago even before I started taking drugs—you know I run when I take them. Like barbiturates. I take them but I never really run from anything, because I find myself more depressed and more mentally thinking of suicide. Especially lately, I find myself at points where it's a pain—just not physical but mental. It's a tension through your whole body and your mind. I find myself not knowing what to do, just wanting to grasp anything. Just a tension so bad it hurts and not knowing what I can do about it. I try to talk to someone, but they don't really understand. They don't really know the feeling. You can't really explain how you feel, and they can't do anything for you, so you just find yourself taking speed, barbs, or anything to bring you out of that, but you end up right back in the same depressed situation that you were in before, and twice as many problems.

I just want to change the whole thing. I don't want to take drugs any more. I just want to get myself to feeling better. I am run-down and sick. If I don't take them I will be really depressed, and my whole body is just worn out, and I don't feel like doing anything. I know that a long time ago I was depressed without drugs, but at least I felt better. I felt more like doing things. Any more it seems like anybody—that's all they ever do is with drugs. Everything they do, they take a drug. I can't handle them any more. Some way I've got to change it. I've talked to a lot of counselors. I'll go to them and I'll try to talk to them but I feel like there is no communication, so I just won't go back. Right now I feel that I've tried everything outside counseling——

Counselor:	(*Interrupting.*) Could you state who you were seeing and how many times? What was the longest time you saw someone?
Client:	I've communicated with Dr. Jones a lot. He's my mother's psychiatrist. He's been with me since—he's the one that admitted me to the hospital when I was sixteen. Dr. Salzman, from the University Hospital, is the one that said I should get away from everything and that it would help a lot. Lately I've had some interviews at the Drug Rehabilitation on the South Side, and I went over to a clinic on the East Side. I talked to them, and they

sent me back to the one on the South Side across from the hospital. I only saw a counselor once. I talked to her on the phone. I go there once and I know what I want to do, but when I'm out, when I'm at home, I stop for a while, but it slowly comes all back—you know, the same people—and I'm right back where I was. It just doesn't do any good.

Counselor: Tell me a little bit about your family situation.

Client: I'm living with myself and my two children, but there are friends that come over a lot. . . . I know I've had a lot of family problems at home. Like I've had a lot of problems with my mother and my father—emotional. I've never done anything to my children. I've never come to the point of harming them. If I get like right now, I just went like kind of on a binge, I send them over with my mom, and I've been calling her every day and telling her that I feel sick and I'm going to try and do something. I just don't know quite what to do.

Counselor: Are you divorced or separated?

Client: Separated. I went to legal services, and it was paid for, but I've missed court about three times. I've wanted a divorce, but there are so many things, I just never get them done. I just never get around to it, and I always fall back. I fall into a rut mostly. It's just so hard to explain. I really don't know what's wrong or what the problem is, but I know that for me to do this, there has got to be something. (*Crying.*)

Counselor: Could you tell me a little about your suicidal thoughts and feelings?

Client: I just feel that I'm not going anywhere. I always think that things will get better, but they never get better, they always get worse and I feel it's just going to go on like this for the rest of my life. And if this is all I have to look forward to, I just as soon not be here. I just think if I wasn't here, my children would be better off, because I don't know what I'm going to do. If I'm in this condition, I'm in no condition to bring them up. I don't want to see them ever take drugs or be in the predicament I'm in. I wouldn't want to see that, and if I can't handle it myself, they aren't going to be able to either. They are going to end up with a mental problem or some type of a problem themselves, and I don't want to see that.

Counselor: Could you tell me about your visit to the County Hospital this afternoon and what happened there?

Client: Well, I went in. I had been pretty low and crying all day. I don't like that hospital. I had been in there once before and they transferred me to the University. I just went in to get an antibiotic . . . I was going to have this guy I have been going out with pick me up this morning and take me in there. . . .

Counselor: Did you have a psychiatric evaluation?

Client: No. I didn't go into the mental ward. I just went for the antibiotic into the walk-in.

Counselor: So you weren't evaluated psychiatrically this afternoon?

Client: No. I didn't want to go to that hospital. I don't know what I was going to do. Patsy [a friend] out here has been trying to help me decide. We called up and questioned a psychiatrist, Dr. Arnold, and he said the way it sounded to him, it probably would be better if I would admit myself for a while until I got a little stronger and then had outside counseling afterwards. Right now I don't know where I would go, because I don't know anyone but Patsy that doesn't take drugs.

Counselor: Then when was the time you saw Dr. Arnold, or called him?

Client: I called him today, just before we came over here. My mother called here and she talked to another psychiatrist. If I was going to admit myself, I wasn't going to the County Hospital. I know I have to do something, because every time I go out I know I'm going to do it again. I don't think my will power is as strong as it was before.

Counselor: Why did you come in particularly today instead of yesterday or tomorrow?

Client: Probably because I had stopped by and I was looking around at everybody and I was thinking a lot about everything. I had talked to my mother and my little kids on the phone, and a friend of mine was seen here a little while ago. I don't think she was as bad . . . but she's dead now. I don't know if it was an accident or she was suicidal. They said it was accidental, out at Blue River Gorge. I was just looking around at everybody I knew and at myself. I'm looking for someone to tell me what to do for help. I don't know what to do. I don't know anybody else, like friends. A lot of people are into it so bad they don't understand, so I just push it away and say it's not there. I'm fooling myself—you know—there's nothing wrong with me. But I know there is. There has to be something wrong with me if I do this stuff to myself.

Counselor: Do you have a habit now?

Client: I don't know. I think it's psychologically maybe more than physically. I don't think I do. I've been hitting up barbs. I might go through a little bit of cramps. I've gone through a little bit of stomach cramps before, but nothing I can't handle. I took barbiturates last night, but I haven't taken anything today. Last night I didn't hit the barbs, I dropped them so I could sleep. I think it's more mental addiction than physical addiction.

Counselor: Have you been to General Hospital at all with this?

Client: Not the hospital. I haven't been in the hospital with it. I have a physical doctor. He's kind of also been my counselor too. I start to talk to someone, but I never really get anywhere. I start thinking things like, they really don't understand or they don't know, and then I run from them too and it's just a waste of time. That's always how it ends.

Counselor excuses herself to consult. How would you diagram the case?

130

DEDUCTIVE MODEL

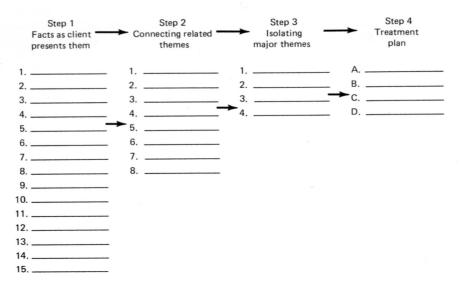

Step 1
Facts as client
presents them

Step 2
Connecting related
themes

Step 3
Isolating
major themes

Step 4
Treatment
plan

Step 1	Step 2	Step 3	Step 4
1. _____	1. _____	1. _____	A. _____
2. _____	2. _____	2. _____	B. _____
3. _____	3. _____	3. _____	C. _____
4. _____	4. _____	4. _____	D. _____
5. _____	5. _____		
6. _____	6. _____		
7. _____	7. _____		
8. _____	8. _____		
9. _____			
10. _____			
11. _____			
12. _____			
13. _____			
14. _____			
15. _____			

Additional comments:

Step 1
Facts as Client Presents Them

drug use since 16
hospitalized
change environment
no sense to living
returned, quit school
pregnant, married
separated
pregnant again, reunited
separated
boy, girl
stopped drugs for a while
husband, drug user
repeated attempts to quit
can't
on probation
environment
past 5 years, bad
problems and drugs
parent problems
kids safe, with parents
separated, can't follow
thru
suicidal potential
contacting resources
suicide of friend
tell me what to do
run from problems

Additional Information
medical problems
family calls
friend outside
pills yesterday
calls to psychiatrists

Step 2
Connecting Related Themes

Drug History
—since 16
—repeated attempts to quit
—husband user
—environmental influences
—"dropped" yesterday

Recent events
—suicide of friend
—very depressed
—losses
—talk with family
—medical problems

Feels
—no sense to living
—loss of hope
—trapped
—alone/isolated
—guilt; kids, life pattern

Strengths
—asking for help
—some insight
—has tried to change
—welfare of kids
—on probation
—had stopped drugs before

Mental Status
—oriented x3
—drug influenced
—mood and affect
—suicidal ideation

Step 3
Isolating Major Themes

Crisis situation
—events
—verbal report
—behavior
—feelings

Coping skills
—drugs
—repeated failure to stop
—poor environmental supports
—feels she can't

Connected themes
—depression and loss
—unstable life pattern
—outpatient counseling a failure
—trapped and hopelessness

Step 4
Treatment Plan

Evaluate for immediate hospitalization

Medical check due to drug usage

Help notify significant others

Arrange for transfer to appropriate hospital

Discussion

The psychiatrist on call at the hospital was consulted for immediate evaluation for admission to the psychiatric unit. Since the client resided outside the hospital's catchment area, the crisis counselor and the psychiatrist worked together to get the client admitted to a hospital that served the area in which she lived. The client's friend, who had been waiting for her in a car, drove her to the hospital, where she was admitted by prearrangement. She remained as an inpatient for two weeks.

A transcript cannot fully convey the flat effect and depressed mood that Sandy expressed during this interview. She spoke in a monotone and showed little voice inflection irrespective of the content. At one point she cried a little. But the general response was unemotional. When she described her suicidal thoughts and plans, her voice was hollow and lifeless. When she spoke of her children and how they would be better off without her, she showed no feeling of aversiveness toward death. Severe depression and apparent resignation to death in combination with the suicidal content and lack of community supports made hospitalization the most appropriate consideration.

Some elements in this interview which might have clouded the counselor's judgment were the client's report of chronic drug use, her admission that she had recently "dropped" some "reds," and her indication that she had found counseling of little help. Clients with these characteristics typically turn counselors off. They usually show little if any gain in therapy, frequently attempt to manipulate the counselor, show little objective behavior change, and often become sources of frustration to those who attempt to help them. Had the counselor allowed these biasing factors to interfere with her clinical knowledge concerning drug use, depression, loss, and suicidal potential in regard to Sandy, the client might not have been hospitalized. Instead, the counselor might well have interpreted her complaints as one more attempt to manipulate those about her. In this event, she might have been referred to another outpatient counseling facility. Such an action would have entailed an unnecessary degree of risk for this potentially suicidal client.

As is frequently the case with chronic drug users, Sandy became a victim of her environmental influences: friends, relatives, and other drug-users. In addition, the drugs provided a certain amount of temporary psychological relief from the anxieties and stress that she experienced prior to drug use. As this case exemplifies, a self-defeating, self-perpetuating pattern is frequently observed in which the client finds himself or herself in a drug trap, pursuing short-term relief from psychological pain through dangerous habituating and illegal activities. Such clients require appropriate and effective problem-solving techniques to cope with stressful conditions in their lives. Their needs are as valid and as legitimate as anyone else's, and the crisis counselor must not dismiss such clients as hopeless or expendable from a clinical viewpoint. This is particularly true when assessing for self-destructive and suicidal potential in which there is a high risk of imminent danger.

In conclusion, some comments about the conduct of the interview are appropriate. For the most part, open- and closed-end questions were used appropriately, and the counselor was facilitative in her requests for more information. She focused when necessary for more specific information. And only in a few places did she ask more than one question at a time. She offered only as much structure as was necessary to get a full picture of the nature of the crisis and essentially succeeded in obtaining the information that we recommended be collected during the first interview. It was from these details that the counselor was able to extract the essential elements of the case and develop an appropriate intervention plan.

Suggested Readings

Clauson, J.A. "Drug Use." In *Contemporary Social Problems* (Eds. R.K. Merton and R. Nesbit). New York: Harcourt Brace Jovanovich, 1971.

Group for the Advancement of Psychiatry. *Drug Misuse, A Psychiatric View of a Modern Dilemma.* New York: Charles Scribners and Sons, 1971.

Lester, G., and D. Lester. *Suicide, the Gamble with Death.* Englewood Cliffs, N.J.: Prentice-Hall, 1971.

Meerloo, J.A.M. "Hidden Suicide." In *Suicidal Behaviors, Diagnosis and Management* (Ed. H.L.P. Resnik). Boston: Little, Brown, 1968.

Moss, L.M., and D.M. Hamilton. "Psychotherapy of the Suicidal Patient." In *Clues to Suicide* (Eds. E.S. Shneidman and N.L. Farberow). New York: McGraw-Hill, 1957.

Murphey, G.E., and E. Robins. "The Communication of Suicidal Ideas." In *Suicidal Behaviors, Diagnosis and Management* (Ed. H.L.P. Resnik). Boston: Little, Brown, 1968.

Pope, H. *Voices from the Drug Culture.* Boston: Beacon Press, 1971.

Resnik, H.L.P., ed. *Suicidal Behaviors, Diagnosis and Management.* Boston: Little, Brown, 1968.

Shneidman, E.S., and N.L. Farberow, eds. *Clues to Suicide.* New York: McGraw-Hill, 1957.

Sutter, A.G. "Worlds of Drug Use on the Street Scene." In *Delinquency, Crime and Social Process* (Eds. D. Cessey and D. Ward). New York: Harper & Row, 1969.

12 "The Evil Smell"

Shirley, a young woman of twenty-three, was referred for crisis counseling by a local hospital after being seen in the emergency room with a complaint of being unable to breathe. She was in a reported state of panic, certain that her lungs were about to collapse. The next day, accompanied by her aunt, she arrived at a Mental Health Center. She appeared calm, neatly dressed, and cooperative as she entered the office, showing no indication of being unusually upset.

Counselor: Tell me why you are here today, Shirley.

Client: I've been so upset and I've had an emotional shock really, partly because my leg has been lengthened and all my life it has been shorter than my right one. And then past problems too.

Counselor: What was it that brought you in today in particular?

Client: I went to Valley Hospital and they advised me to come here.

Counselor: Why was that?

Client: Because everything was so upsetting to me.

Counselor: Why did you go to the hospital last night?

Client: Because I was so upset and I couldn't hardly breathe. I felt like my lungs were going to collapse or something. And every time I hear the sound of *s*'s it's like a shrill. And I was upset before. I had gone there the day before yesterday, and I was blowing my nose real hard to get the rest of it out—it was all dry inside my nose. Then something popped inside my ear, and then I started feeling worse.

Counselor: What do you mean upset?

Client: Just past experiences and the shock of my leg on top of it.

Counselor: What are your past experiences?

Client: Well, my father was trying to make advances, and I felt that I had to, because I didn't know what he would do to me. I have always been afraid of him because he talks real loud and he has always harped on me—"Do it this way, do it that way"—you know. He says that he was only trying to teach me how to do it.

Counselor: What do you mean *it*? Sex?

Client: Yes. I left home a couple of years ago because of this. He started in again and made me promise not to tell my mother. When he did it the first time, my mother was in the Midwest with my sick grandfather. He had cancer of the brain. My dad started in then, and he made me promise not to tell her after she had come home . . . because he would just deny the whole story.

135

Counselor:	What happened yesterday that made you feel so upset?
Client:	I kept seeing visions of the devil. Day before yesterday I went in the bathroom, and I looked in the mirror and it was red, you know. Like a cat's face. And yesterday it was black, and thoughts kept going through my mind.
Counselor:	Thoughts of . . . .
Client:	Just bad things, like talking real sharp to everybody and just being real mean. . . . The more I talked about it, the worse it got. I started to panic and couldn't breathe, and my chest started hurting, and my stomach started getting sick, and I was getting headaches. But all this has gotten worse since that thing popped in my ear.
Counselor:	What finally made you decide to go to the hospital last night?
Client:	My thoughts weren't straight. They were confused. I kept getting a prophecy, and I kept writing down everything that came to my mind. My aunt says that that's not right. So she called a pastor. So I talked to him, and then when I got real bad he came over and tried to talk to me about it some more. Then I felt at peace about it and went to sleep, but then the next morning I was back the same way again. . . . Just like the devil was on the outside of me this time—you know—and he was trying to get in there and taunt me of those pasts that I have had.
Counselor:	Could you see him?
Client:	Well, not clearly.
Counselor:	Could you hear him?
Client:	The voice was the thoughts.
Counselor:	Were the voices coming from inside or from outside?
Client:	From inside.
Counselor:	What were they saying?
Client:	I can't even remember now. (*Pause.*)
Counselor:	You said that your thoughts were confused and you were getting prophecies. What kind of prophecies?
Client:	That my parents were going to get a divorce, and for me to get there and to look in my dad's face, and he would apologize to me for all that he had done and that he wants my legs to be just as normal as any other child's.
Counselor:	And this came in prophecies?
Client:	Yes. And my prophecy somewhere towards the middle told me to go in the bathroom and look in the mirror. So I went in and looked in the mirror and that's when I saw the red eagle and I started seeing that black eagle right before my eyes. Since I saw that eagle my head has just been swimming. Last night the cat wanted in the front door, so I went and opened the front door, and it felt like

somebody was pushing that door and pushing me out of that house.

Counselor: That was last night?

Client: Yes.

Counselor: How did you react to that?

Client: I said, "Dad, will you get out of here," and I went and laid down and I felt better.

Counselor: Then what happened?

Client: Then I felt better and I ate almost a normal full dinner and it really tasted good after the last few days. Then all of a sudden it tasted like water. Then I got all upset.

Counselor: What happened when you got all upset?

Client: It was hard to breathe and I just told him I couldn't take any more.

Counselor: Couldn't take any more what?

Client: All of this upsetness. Sometimes I get real cold chills like I can't get warm enough and I get real annoyed. . . . I have been going to Bible studies and trying to get myself straightened out.

Counselor: Where do you go for Bible Studies?

Client: This lady, Sally, has Bible studies on Wednesdays and it's just for women. We just pray and visit and sing special songs. On Friday nights we go to Sally's again and Al, this teacher, he goes to her house and teaches us about the Bible and everything. That's for men and women both. I was feeling really happy and perky and everything. And then one Friday night about two or three weeks ago, I was just standing there, and I kept thinking something was wrong a few days before, and then something popped into my head: "Oh, pray to the Lord that you are going to be healed." So I did and my aunt, hearing that, felt the Lord was going to heal my legs. I felt that he was going to heal me inside. So I prayed for that, and my aunt prayed for my legs. All of it has just hit me all at once.

Counselor: How has it hit you?

Client: Well, one night I was laying in a bed and praying to the Lord that He would heal my legs because I felt sure that He would. All of a sudden I felt a transformation of life like I was just going back. Then last Tuesday my aunt went to Bible study, and I was at home by myself with her son. All of a sudden something came over me and I was playing the part of a baby and other times I was playing the part of Jesus, and all of a sudden I was playing the part of a baby myself . . . and these smells I have been getting.

Counselor: What kind of smells?

Client: Like smells of evil or something.

Counselor: What does it smell like?

Client: Like a burning or something or kind of an evil smell. Before all this had started I kept getting all these chills. I couldn't get warm enough.

Counselor: And then you started smelling evil? How did you know it was evil that you smelled?

Client: I don't even know if it was evil or not. It was just that awful smell. I just couldn't stand it.

Counselor: What did it smell like?

Client: Oh. . . . (*Long pause.*)

Counselor: Have you ever smelled it before?

Client: No.

Counselor: How do you know it smelled awful?

Client: It was just like a mass growth or something. It was like a sickening smell. When I lay down I feel much better than when I'm sitting up. Then I get these panics when I breathe real hard and my chest hurts, and it feels like my arms are going to collapse, and I felt like my heart was going to stop at the hospital last night. I kept getting these pains in my hips and my legs and a real cold tingling all over my legs as if He was healing my legs even more. Even my aunt says my legs are both the same length now. She said possibly that's part of the reason I've been so upset because of the shock, because I've had this all my life.

Counselor: What is it that you've had all your life?

Client: Clubfeet, and I've had about five operations altogether. The doctors told me there is nothing more that they could do when they discharged me. The last operation I had was when I was in the eighth grade.

Counselor: And your one leg was shorter then than the other?

Client: Yes.

Counselor: And you think you've noticed a change in them?

Client: Yes, and this friend said that she could see a difference, and my aunt has checked it too. She feels both my legs are the same length now too. I keep having an urge to call my parents, and felt they were rejecting me because of my Christianity. I had felt so burdened for them, like they are in desperate need and the Lord is really dealing with them so they will be saved and be happy.

Counselor: Did you call your parents?

Client: Yes. I called my dad night before last and my mom was working and my brother answered, and he sounded different—like he was full of joy that he never had before. I just told my father that I had a greater love for them than I ever felt before since I've moved here. The Lord has just given me so much courage just to be able to get in the car and drive, and I have never even been able to face the fact that I had enough mind and knowledge to pass the permit test, and I actually passed it, about three weeks ago. As long as I'm not nervous or anything, I can just drive that car like it's nothing. Then when my aunt started taking me out in the city with all the signals and traffic and everything, then I started panicking again. Before, I kept imagining my dad sitting next to me yelling at me and not having any patience with me. He says, "When you learn how to drive you are going to do it this way and under my conditions, so that you will know everything about the car."

Counselor: So when you were driving you felt like your dad was there?

Client: I felt him though I didn't see him, because I would get that awful smell again.

Counselor: And that was how you knew he was there?

Client: Yes. And I'd pray to the Lord to show me the difference between the Lord speaking to me, and the devil speaking to me. I told the Lord that I didn't want the devil at all.

Counselor: You don't know which one is which?

Client: Right. So I asked him to let me know and tell me which way was right.

Counselor: And did he?

Client: I'm still confused. The different situations go back and forth. My thoughts one minute say it's the Lord speaking to me when there are all these shrill *s*'s and that is the Lord, and still other times, when it's real quiet, that that is the Lord and these evil things keep coming in my mind at both times, so I still don't know which is which.

Counselor: What do you mean by shrill *s*'s? I don't quite understand.

Client: *S*'s, like it's echoing.

Counselor: The letter *s* you mean?

Client: Yes, and sometimes *d*'s and *t*'s. All this has really hit me when I blew my nose and something hard went like this—like it was going to pop out of my ear and then it plugged up again.

Counselor: And that's when you started hearing the *s*'s, and *d*'s, and *t*'s?

Client: Yes.

Counselor: How did you feel when you woke up this morning?

Client: I don't know. I just felt scared, because I didn't know what was going to happen.

Counselor: Was it the same kind of scared that you had felt before?

Client: Yes. Then I felt the more I talked about it—you know, without any medication or anything—then the better I felt. And I felt if my dad would just apologize to me for what he has done, that I would be at peace. I told my aunt that what the Lord told me to do is to see my dad and for him to apologize, and I felt like he had never loved me before until I talked to him night before last.

Counselor:	And you felt like he loved you then?
Client:	Yes.
Counselor:	What did he say to make you feel that way?
Client:	He just said that he loved me no matter what happened to me. . . . Even though he felt that I was doing things that were wrong to him, that it just made him happy because it made me happy, and so he was happy then.
Counselor:	What did he feel you were doing that was wrong by him?
Client:	I don't know. He has never told me. He said it was about a half a dozen things.
Counselor:	He told you this the other night when you talked to him on the phone?
Client:	Yes. He told me he would just deny it if I told anybody about it because he was afraid it would break up the family.
Counselor:	Did you have sex with your father?
Client:	We never did go all the way. He was just doing everything else.
Counselor:	Like what? Touching?
Client:	Yes. But he told me that he didn't go all the way because he was afraid that I might get pregnant . . . and he told me later that if I got my own apartment, got a job, was able to support myself living by myself, then he could go to the apartment by himself and teach me how so that I would know what to guard against like if I ever went out with guys—so that I would know what to be aware of.
Counselor:	How old were you when this first started?
Client:	I was in business college.
Counselor:	How many years did you live at home under these conditions?
Client:	I'm not even sure. About a year or two.
Counselor:	Do you go out with boys?
Client:	No. I had a boyfriend when I was going to mental therapy, and we were going together for nine months, and he asked me to marry him. I saved all the money I could, and I even did without so that we could have more money when we got married. He wanted me to go to England with him and live with him. He said that when he first saw me his problem . . . was that he revealed himself to little children. . . . He had been ordered by the court to go to this mental therapy, and he told me that he loved me for what I was and I was helping him and he wasn't even doing it any more because of me. And here I didn't even know I was helping him. Then all of a sudden out of a clear blue sky he just hung up. No explanation, no nothing.
Counselor:	How long ago was that?
Client:	About five months before I moved here. . . . I've been trying to find a full-time job so I can really be independent of others.

Counselor: What do you think we can do for you here?

Client: I don't know. Just that I've been referred here and that I need help. That's all I know.

Counselor: How do you think you need help.

Client: Mentally I guess. (*Pause.*) But I feel that if my dad would just apologize and accept the Lord that I would be at complete peace. . . . My aunt said that I should ask the Lord for forgiveness if I was going to be able to forgive my stepdad for this because he might be mentally ill. So I prayed to the Lord and told the Lord that I did forgive him.

Counselor: Do you feel guilty?

Client: (*Pause.*) Well, I feel guilty because I'm telling people about all this when it might make my family get a divorce—you know. I've always felt that people wouldn't accept me because of my past, so I feel that everywhere I go I've got to tell them so that they will accept me.

Counselor: I see. And do they accept you?

Client: Yes, and I didn't realize it. And I told my Grandma Alice, and she said we figured your dad might be mentally ill because he had done this to my sister too. And in that prophecy that I had—it was about ten pages long it seemed like—he was performing blasphemy against his son. He was going to be endangering my mother's life.

Counselor: This was in the prophecy that you got?

Client: Yes. And to get some money out as soon as I could afford it so that she could take me back and see them so that when my dad saw my legs and how happy I was, that I would be at peace. I just kept having the urge and I kept telling my aunt and my uncle that they had to get my parents here. I feel that the sooner they accept the Lord, then the better I will be.

At this point the counselor excuses herself to consult. How would you diagram the case?

142

DEDUCTIVE MODEL

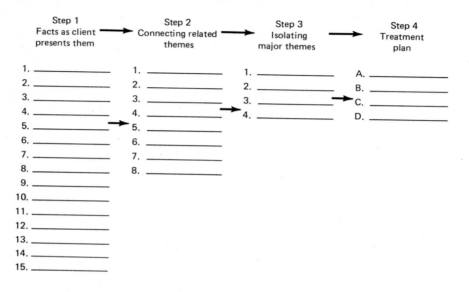

Step 1	Step 2	Step 3	Step 4
Facts as client presents them	Connecting related themes	Isolating major themes	Treatment plan

Additional comments:

Step 1

upset
leg lengthened
past problems
hospital referred
sound of S's
something popped
father's advances
sexual
visions of the devil
bad things
thoughts weren't straight
getting prophecy
devil taunting
hallucinations; visual
food taste like water
thoughts of parents upsetting
here two months with aunt
Bible studies
leg healing
psychotic?, Jesus, baby
smells evil
driving and father
lost job
get away
chills
past week, bad
devil with me, smell
lord and devil
talk and feel better
dad to apologize
sex with father
business college
boyfriend, previous therapy
stepfather, not real father?
dad sick

Additional Information

Steps 2 and 3 Combined

mental status
–hearing voices
–seeing things
–smelling things
–tasting things
–delusional system
–sexual material
–depersonalization

recent events
–fear of sleep
–hospital visit
–talk with parents
–healing of leg
–panicky
–prophecy
–confused thoughts
–more psychotic material
–disturbed sleep

feels
–overwhelmed
–guilty
–fearful
–unexplained feelings

coping skills
–not an apparent danger to self/others
–previous counseling
–family support; aunt
–Bible study; friends

Intervention Plan

1. Refer to psychiatrist for medication evaluation.

2. Talk with aunt regarding her opinion. Will she feel comfortable with Shirley at home while the medication takes effect?

3. Set up appointment for a few days hence. Check on meds and mental status.

4. Initiate referral to a day-care program.

Discussion

The psychiatrist who evaluated Shirley for medication put her on Mellaril, a major tranquilizer designed to help in the management of psychotic disorders and symptoms. The counselor then spoke with the supervisor of the mental health center's day-care program, who made an immediate appointment to see Shirley and evaluate her for their program. The day-care concept is a closely supervised treatment program that has been devised as an alternative approach to inpatient hospitalization. Candidates for this service spend anywhere from a few hours to several days a week participating in group activities, such as counseling and enhancement of their social and task-orientated skills. This program was carefully explained to Shirley and her relatives with whom she was living. Everyone accepted the plan and agreed to continue to provide supervision and transportation to the center during this crisis period. A follow-up contact two weeks later confirmed that she was still in the program. However, one week later Shirley left the city and returned to live with her parents.

Interviewing a person in crisis who presents psychotic and "crazy" material often is a very anxiety-producing experience. The inexperienced counselor tends to fear that if he is not careful or asks the wrong question, he may cause the client to become even more psychotic. Worse yet, he may incite the client to become violent. This, in fact, rarely occurs, unless it is with someone who is quite paranoid, and even then it is the exception rather than the rule. If the counselor pays close attention to the cues and signals that the client produces, indicating a state of irritation and agitation, there is little chance he will unwittingly provoke the client. Such body language as extreme movement, gesturing and posturing, wringing and shaking of the hands, alternately crying and laughing, and other agitated responses to the crisis situation should alert the counselor to the potential disturbing state of the client. In addition, the counselor should pay careful attention to the specific responses elicited from the client when the counselor explores particular areas. Counseling with a potentially psychotic client requires that the counselor observe closely the manner in which the client responds to the questions asked by the counselor or family member. In this context, also pay attention to such physiological cues as excessive sweating, color and flush of the face, rate and speed of breathing, etc.

Note also the manner in which the client answers the counselor's request for information. If, for example, the counselor notices that the client wanders in his answer or brings up some bizarre or grossly unrelated material, this should signal the counselor to become more structured in his interviewing approach. If, in addition to these loose associations in the client's responses, there is substantial evidence of very powerful emotionality, the counselor should begin to suspect a possible psychotic condition. Yet the same suspicion ought to be aroused when the client is so devoid of affect and emotional expression that he severely underplays the importance of obviously critical occurrences in his life.

The counselor must seek to avoid needless agitation of a severely disturbed client. It is not necessary to encourage such a client to ramble on endlessly without a specific purpose in mind other than expression for its own sake. The excessive provocation of an already severely disturbed person may actually contribute to his decompensation, the very outcome the crisis counselor is committed to prevent.

In the case of Shirley, the counselor had little prior information that would have prepared her for what developed during the interview. Crisis counseling frequently involves an element of surprise. The presenting problems may not always truly reflect what the counselor will actually see in the interview. While this is a time-honored principle with all forms of counseling and psychotherapy, it is particularly true in crisis work. While we do not advocate that every counselor be prepared for the worst, we do underscore vigilance and the ability to shift techniques to refocus the course of the interview in accordance with the needs of the client. On more than one occasion a client has presented himself as being in a moderate state of crisis when in actuality he was severely disturbed, revealing homicidal, suicidal, or psychotic material. Even all the preparatory information that the counselor may have prior to seeing the client (see Chapter 5) may not be sufficient. A flexible stance and the ability to deal with surprises is thus a valuable skill. Simply having a concern for people and caring for them, in our view, is not enough. A combination of human concern, technical skill, and good judgment distinguishes the successful crisis counselor.

The reader should take careful note of the way in which this counselor conducted the interview. To begin with, note how she used a combination of open- and closed-end questions in accordance with needs of the immediate situation. A good example of the open-end approach is the question "What do you mean upset?" And then, shortly after that: "What are your past experiences?" Notice on the other hand that the counselor did not overuse the open-end question. Most of her questions were designed to secure specific information pertaining to the immediate crisis. For example, she asks, "Why did you go to the hospital last night?" and then, "How have you been sleeping the last few nights?"

There are also sequences of questions in which the counselor sets the tone of the interview; questions that tell the client that structure is the mode of interaction. Note the series of questions beginning with: "Could you see him?" and ending with: "What happened when you got all upset?" Having secured the necessary information, the counselor then shifted back to a more open-end approach, confident that the client could discuss the material without undue stress. Furthermore, the counselor saw no advantage in dwelling upon the specifics of the hallucinatory and delusional material. A further analysis of this material itself might have been more appropriate in a less emergent situation, but not in a crisis interview.

The skillful use of bridging techniques can be found at several points in the interview: "Thoughts of . . . ?" and "What kind of smells?" Then notice how the client is able to respond to these rather minimal cues to continue. This use of bridging also tells the counselor how well able the client is to deal with the content. In addition, it suggests to the counselor just how much structure to offer the client in the future. Remember, one of the goals is to encourage the client to develop his story at his own pace and without too much interference from the counselor. When the client is able to handle the kinds of subtle signals this counselor offers, the counselor learns a little more about his client's mental state. This, in turn, influences the kind of treatment intervention plan that the counselor will be offering his client. If everyone who presented psychotic material were to be placed in a hospital, our mental health facilities would be even more overtaxed than they are now. And there is ample research indicating that hospitalization need not always be considered the primary mode of intervention (Mendel and Green 1967).

One question that was never cleared up during the course of the interview was whether the client's father was her natural father or her stepfather. It was learned later that he was her stepfather. This fact might well have been clarified at the time of the interview, as it alters our perception of the problem. The incest taboo may have evoked anxiety in the counselor leading her to over-emphasize the psychotic content. A further point needing clarification is whether the sexual events did in fact take place or whether they were part of the client's psychotic delusional system. The counselor reports that by the time the stepfather information came out she was rather overwhelmed with what material she already had and didn't think to clarify it. The sense of being overwhelmed in a case like this is a fairly typical response by crisis workers regardless of their experience.

Two final comments. First, the counselor did not inquire into the possibility of this client being a danger to herself or others, and that was an oversight. While it is not always necessary to get into the specific question of "how suicidal are you?" the counselor would have been well advised to learn more about how the client handled herself when besieged by the evil forces she described. The second point is that the counselor should have considered bringing the relative into a more active role during the evaluation and treatment process. This could have been accomplished by perhaps interviewing Shirley and her aunt together initially. If this proved too much for the client, then they could have been interviewed separately. If the counselor could not see them conjointly, then at least she could have spent time with the aunt—in a collateral way—in a separate interview. This could very well have added some factual data to those areas of discrepancy mentioned earlier. Whenever possible and appropriate, the counselor should include friends and close relatives in the crisis intervention plan. In fact, their inclusion may often provide the additional support needed to enable the client in crisis to mobilize his or her resources more fully (Getz et al. 1974). As it turned out, that was what happened in this case with regard to transportation and supervision of medication. As a final note, you may recall Beck's (1971) frequent failure to locate a specific precipitating event among patients diagnosed as schizophrenic. The apparent lack of such an event in Shirley's case may have been useful in making a differential assessment.

References

Beck, J.C., and K. Worthen. "Precipitating Stress, Crisis Theory and Hospital-ization in Schizophrenia and Depression." *Archives of General Psychiatry* 26 (1972): 123-29.

Getz, W.L., B. Fujita, and D. Allen. "The Use of Paraprofessionals in Crisis Intervention: The Evaluation of an Innovative Program." Accepted for publication, *American Journal of Community Psychology*, 1974.

Mendel, W., and G.A. Green. *The Therapeutic Management of Psychological Illness*. New York: Basic Books, 1967.

Suggested Readings

Arieti, S. "Schizophrenia: The Manifest Symptomology, the Psychodynamic and Formal Mechanisms." In *American Handbook of Psychiatry*. Vol. 1. New York: Basic Books, 1959.

Brody, E.B., and F.C. Redlich, eds. *Psychotherapy with Schizophrenics*. New York: International University Press, 1964.

Hill, L.B. *Psychotherapeutic Intervention in Schizophrenia*. Chicago: University of Chicago Press, 1973.

Lidz, T. *The Origin and Treatment of Schizophrenic Disorders*. New York: Basic Books, 1973.

Sarason, I. *Abnormal Psychology*. New York: Appleton-Century-Crofts, 1972.

"Everything's Fine"

The client described in the following pages is Jerry, an eighteen-year-old adolescent who was brought in by several of his friends following the ingestion of an undetermined number of aspirin earlier in the day. The setting is the emergency room of a community hospital. During the course of the single interview, the counselor attempted to isolate and deal with the precipitating events and the nature of the crisis.

Throughout the interview the client was restless and appeared eager to leave. His friends were waiting outside the counselor's office. Jerry refused to allow the counselor to contact anyone even though he was currently living at home and going to high school.

Counselor: Okay, why don't you tell me what happened this afternoon, Jerry.

Client: My younger brother was just in Cleveland, diving in the Nationals, and he came home. My girlfriend and I weren't getting along very good but we had everything all worked out. We are engaged right now and we had everything all worked out . . . and then he came home, and he must have told her something. They won't tell me what they said. She started getting really mad at me and today she told me . . . to just forget it, and she is going to forget about me till I grow up. She doesn't want to have anything to do with me. She went on and on. This was about 10:00 a.m. Then she left at 11:00 and came back at 2:00, and talked, and then she told me she didn't want to talk anymore. I was at school doing some work and she came back at 4:00 and I saw her, and she asked why I was still hanging around. I told her I was doing some homework, and she said, "Will you just leave it. I don't want to see you ever again." So I got kind of upset. Then I went home and my parents got really on me. They go, "You shouldn't care about her anyway" and start saying all this bad stuff. They said, "You should start thinking about your goals and stop worrying about all this stuff." I said, "Just forget it, I don't care about anything." Then I went in the bathroom and took a bunch of pills. It sounds stupid now, but right then it was just about the only thing to do.

Counselor: What do you think your brother might have said to your girlfriend?

Client: I don't know. I don't know what happened. All of a sudden everything was just all goofed up. Jim won't tell me what he said. . . .

Counselor:	Why do you think something was said?
Client:	Because she said, "After what Jim told me, I understand now why you are the way you are," and all this stuff. I don't know what he said. Before he left we weren't getting along and he knew it. He didn't realize that we had figured everything out.
Counselor:	Everything like what?
Client:	I went out with this girl one time. I asked her permission. We weren't really going out. We were just going to this group thing called Young Life. It's like when you get together and sing. I asked her if I could go with this girl and she said fine. So that night she went out with this guy. She didn't ask or anything. It didn't really bug me or anything, but she said if you can go out with a girl, then I don't see why I can't go out, so we had quite a disagreement. My brother knew all about that, and he thought everything was all screwed up. He's a sophomore at our school. He didn't know everything was all right, and it just turned into a big mess.
Counselor:	How does he know your girlfriend?
Client:	Because she's always at our house, every day, except for today. We have been going together for three and a half years, so it's been quite a while and he knows her real well.
Counselor:	Have you had problems like this before?
Client:	No. The first two years we didn't argue. Everything was just great, you know. We haven't broken up at any time. It's just been a really neat relationship. We both understand each other—at least I thought we did. But I don't know.
Counselor:	And recently?
Client:	I guess it's all right. I don't know why it would change. After I did it I called my friends that are out there, and they said don't worry, girls are like that. So I'm not going to do that again.
Counselor:	Let me kind of get the sequences straight this afternoon. You went over to see your girlfriend?
Client:	You mean this morning? No, we were at school and during second period we were together. She was talking to me and telling me that everything was all over—and she was tired of me being the way I am. Then we talked again third period, and she told me to get lost. Then sixth period she told me to just forget about her and she is going to forget about me, and then later on she told me to leave—she didn't want to see me. I don't know what she wants now. She's not going to find out about this or else she would be mad.
Counselor:	What about right at the time you said you argued with your parents about her?
Client:	Oh, yeah. When I came home from school at about a quarter after

four I was upset. They said all she is is a—they said a few harsh words. They said, "You shouldn't care about her. You should start thinking about goals in life, and going to school, and not worry about this marriage bit," and all this other stuff. It kind of upset me. I didn't know what to say. They just got on me and on me, and I got uptight about everything. I don't think I would have done anything had they not started saying all that. We've gotten along like most people—not perfect. Most parents don't get along perfect, but we get along pretty well.

Counselor: Have you had fights with them about your girlfriend before?

Client: Oh, a couple. Not really fights. They don't like me getting serious.

Counselor: What about your brother? You said you were having some trouble with him, not getting along.

Client: Well, he's really a good student. He went to the Nationals this year and everything. My parents really like him and think that he's better than all the rest of us. He won't admit it, but I think he has developed that image they are putting to him, like you are really good. He's really good-looking and gets all these girls, and so he just puts me down all the time. I feel stupid. I really do. I feel like a dummy.

Counselor: Have you ever done anything like this before?

Client: No. No. No. And I never will again. It's not worth it.

Counselor: Have you thought about it?

Client: No, I never have. Not until now. I have been happy the last three years. I have been really happy, you know. Then all of a sudden I went crazy. I suppose this will teach me a lesson, if nothing else.

Counselor: What do you think made you decide to do it, and made you decide to take pills?

Client: Because I was in the bathroom and I was just going to go to the bathroom. I looked in the cabinet and then I decided. We don't have pills or anything like that that are really dangerous, so all I could find was aspirin. I didn't know what they would do or how many you had to take to do anything. I guess I took a lot, but maybe I didn't want to die all that much or something (laughing).

Counselor: Then what happened right after you took them?

Client: My brother came barging in. He always does when he figures something out. I told my parents, "I just want to die." So he figured it out. He's not stupid. When I went in there and locked the door, he knew what was going on. He went up and got the key to the bathroom. I took handfulls of ten at a time. I swallowed ten pills at a time. Pretty good, huh?

Counselor: How many did you take all together?

Client: Fifty. It sounds like a lot, but all it did was make my ears ring. I'm not hearing very good because my ears are ringing.

Counselor:	Then, when you brother barged in, what happened?
Client:	My parents were downstairs, so they didn't know what we were talking about. He came in and started yelling at me how dumb I am. He said if you want to live, live right and quit worrying about all this other stuff. He got on me.
Counselor:	He was saying the same sort of things your parents were?
Client:	No. He was just telling me it was stupid to try and kill myself, which is stupid, I know. I'll never do it again.
Counselor:	Do your parents know what happened?
Client:	No.
Counselor:	So your brother came in and talked to you. Then what happened? When did he call your friends?
Client:	He just left. He had a diving team workout at 5:00, so he didn't do anything. Then I called Sherman about 7:00 and I didn't feel good at all.
Counselor:	Did he leave before you called Sherman?
Client:	He didn't know what I was going to do. I have two brothers and one sister, and they found out about it when I was talking to Sherm. They like Rhonda and everything, so they were telling me not to worry about it. I guess everything is alright now. I'll find out when I talk to her.
Counselor:	When you called your friend, he came and got you and took you right over here?
Client:	First we called Middle Earth [a drop-in drug-counseling center]. I didn't want to call anybody. I just wanted to forget about the whole thing. First we called Middle Earth and they told us to call the Poison Center. So we called them and I talked to this doctor who said I had to come in for a blood sample or something. So I came in . . .
Counselor:	Okay. What do you usually do when you run up against problems?
Client:	I talk them over, but she wouldn't talk.
Counselor:	You talk mostly just with Rhonda.
Client:	No, with anybody. But nobody was around but my brother, and a lot of good that does. It just seemed like nobody was there to talk to. Everybody was in class or gone somewhere.
Counselor:	If anything like this comes up again that you can't handle, what do you think you would do when there was no one around?
Client:	Call somebody. I'm not going through this ear ringing bit again. It's driving me crazy.
Counselor:	Nothing really serious happened to you this time. . . .
Client:	Don't worry, I won't do it again.
Counselor:	Okay. When things like this come up and you can't get anybody even on the phone, there are resources in the community like the

hotline number and Middle Earth. It's a pretty serious thing even if you didn't mean it at the time. How do you think things are going to work out with Rhonda?

Client: I hope fine. She's just probably kind of mad or something.

Counselor: What do you think you will do?

Client: She'll come back. I know she will. Everything will be fine. I decided that after I told myself I was dumb.

Counselor: Do you have any idea about what sort of thing——

Client: I don't have any idea. I really don't. It's just driving me crazy. I know she's going to tell me when she cools down a little bit, but it's driving me nuts.

Counselor: What about things your brother might have said in the past about you that——

Client: I can't think of a single thing. I just seems stupid to me anyway. He probably had a good reason, but I can't think of what it would be.

Counselor: Why do you think your brother would do something like that?

Client: I don't know. I really don't know, because he has a girlfriend and everything. I don't see why he would try and take her away from me. Unless he was trying to prove he was better than me, but he already knows that. My parents say all the time, "Why aren't you like Jim?" and things like that.

Counselor: Do you think he was angry at you?

Client: No. He wasn't angry at me. He didn't have any reason to be. I'll find out tomorrow.

Counselor: Would you like to have some help in talking to him, or talking to your girlfriend? Some counseling or something?

Client: I'll see how things go and maybe I'll be back tomorrow to talk.

Counselor: It sounds like you and your brother have not been getting along too well for some time.

Client: We don't get along.

Counselor: If it's driving you to these kind of extremes, I think it's something you should talk about. Is there anyone at school that you could talk to that could help you get this straightened out?

Client: I could talk to the counselor. I talk to him all the time. He's a good friend of mine.

Counselor: Okay. I think that would be a good idea . . . and it's not a healthy sort of thing to keep going like this. How about telling your parents?

Client: No. They would be so hurt that it wouldn't be worth telling them. It's my problem really. They would feel like they failed somewhere. I know they would, because that's the way they are.

Counselor: Well, do they understand how much it hurts you when they are always comparing you with your brother?

Client: No. Well, I said something about it, but they said that they don't. They say it doesn't matter, and don't let it bother you, and all this crap.

Counselor: It does bother you, doesn't it?

Client: Well, it would bother anybody.

Counselor: Maybe it would be a good idea to have a counseling session with them too. You can say you won't do it again, but you didn't think you would do it the first time. You might be a lot happier all around if you can communicate your feelings to each other.

Client: I suppose. I won't tell them what happened. I'll just tell them I'm kind of upset about it. I won't say what I did.

Counselor: They might not take it seriously. It might be a good idea to talk it over with the counselor first. Sometimes it's hard to say the things you need to say. Okay? I'll give you those phone numbers.

Counselor excuses herself from the office. How would you diagram the case?

DEDUCTIVE MODEL

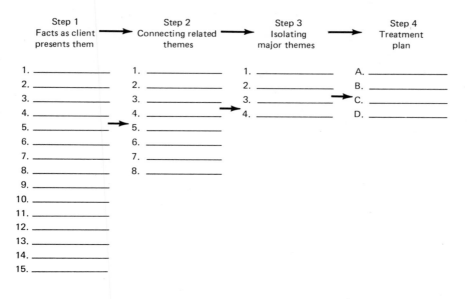

Step 1 Facts as client presents them	Step 2 Connecting related themes	Step 3 Isolating major themes	Step 4 Treatment plan
1.	1.	1.	A.
2.	2.	2.	B.
3.	3.	3.	C.
4.	4.	4.	D.
5.	5.		
6.	6.		
7.	7.		
8.	8.		
9.			
10.			
11.			
12.			
13.			
14.			
15.			

Additional comments:

DEDUCTIVE MODEL

Step 1 Facts as Client Presents Them	*Step 2* Connecting Related Themes	*Step 3* Isolating Major Themes	*Step 4* Treatment Plan

1. bro. athlete
2. girlfriend problems
3. engaged
4. fight at school
5. break up
6. upset
7. parents on me
8. bathroom/pills
9. impulsive
10. what bro. said
11. bro. younger
12. denies prev. prob.
13. parents' response
14. they're to blame
15. competition with bro.
16. "I feel stupid"
17. bro. found him
18. 50 aspirin
19. bro. left
20. called friend
21. 2 bro/1 sister
22. talks about prob.
23. "won't do again"
24. everything fine
25. bro. better than me
26. ambivalence/counsel
27. school counselor
28. hurt by comparison with bro.
29. won't tell parents
	1. **Prec. events**
	  –fight with girlfr.
	  –argument with parents
	  –bro. returning
	
	2. Compared to bro.
	  – by parents
	  – by girlfriend
	  – at school
	  – by peers?
	
	3. Feels
	  –stupid
	  –denies anger
	  –guilty
	  –ambiv/counseling
	  –trapped
	  –threatened
	  –poor self-image
	
	4. History
	  –denies any prev. attempt
	  –many girlfr. fights
	  –chronic rather than acute
	
	5. Family dynamics
	  –achiev. orientated
	  –what kind of communi-
	   cation patterns
	  –much revolves around
	   young, bro.
		1. Anger at significant others which is not being directly expressed.
		
		2. Much need to verbalize without feelings of accompanying guilt.
		
		3. Coping skills include, denial, projection, manipulation, some insight; able to change, questionable at the moment. More like 15 than 18.
		
		4. How much of what he says can be believed?
			1. If possible deal with suicide gesture as an angry and anguished cry for help.
			
			2. Referral to school counselor so he can talk rather than act out his conflicts.
			
			3. Be realistic about referral follow thru.

Discussion

"Adolescence is a period of rapid change affecting both the child's physical make-up and society's expectations regarding his behavior. It is time for looking forward—to new purposes in life, to an occupation, to marriage, to independence from parents, and to a sense of self-identity" (Haimowitz and Haimowitz 1973). It is a period of transition and intense emotional experiences. It is a time of extremes in both mood and behavior. Marked ambivalence, social withdrawal, or antisocial behavior may predominate during this developmental period. Clinicians are frequently heard to comment that there are times during this period of life that are simply chaotic, both for the adolescent and for those who counsel him. Fortunately, the vast majority of adolescents manage to negotiate through this stage and emerge into adulthood with success.

In analyzing this case, several key features should be kept in mind: the nature and seriousness of Jerry's suicide attempt, the message he is communicating, the way the interview was handled, and some general concepts appropriate to work with adolescents.

In the first place, suicidal gesturing in the adolescent must be taken seriously (Hofmann and Becker 1973). While it is seldom possible to predict an adolescent suicide attempt or its consequences, it nevertheless remains for the counselor to pay careful attention to those circumstances that enhance the likelihood of future suicide attempts (Weiner 1970). Twelve percent of all suicide attempts in the U.S. are made by adolescents (Barter, Swaback, and Todd 1968). In this case, it would seem rather clear that Jerry feels trapped between his younger, more successful brother and his parents, who compare him with his brother. We might also speculate that there is some peer pressure involved here, further adding to this feeling and reducing his self-esteem. Frequently, siblings who attend the same school will be unwittingly or purposely compared by teachers, particularly if one sibling is more outstanding in some way than the other.

Adding these several features together, we come up with a composite picture of a threatened, confused, and insecure young man. From the interview we do not know what additional forces may be putting stress on Jerry other than the loss of his girlfriend and the above-mentioned factors. However, these features present sufficient evidence for the counselor to determine that Jerry is in a crisis, whether he recognizes it or not. The seriousness of the suicide threat remains unclear, even given the information that the counselor secured. The impulsiveness with which Jerry took the pills must certainly be considered; however, if a counselor were to hospitalize every adolescent who took a bottle of pills on "impulse," the hospitals would certainly be full. Weinberg found that suicide attempts in hospitals, for example, were closely correlated with the recent loss of a significant other, such as the breakup of a friendship (1970). This would certainly fit in Jerry's case.

What the transcript can not capture, however, is his mood and affect. Jerry said later he was quite eager to leave the interview and get back to his friends who were waiting outside in the hallway. In addition, he was rather giggly and his mood was elevated. He gave the counselor the impression that he was having a rather good time through all this. In addition, he refused to allow the counselor to contact his parents or anyone else, thus giving the impression that there was a considerable amount of manipulation going on by him against Rhonda, his brother, parents, and peers.

Any time there is a suicide gesture with similar attending circumstances, the counselor must be alert to the possibility of manipulation as the major factor rather than a strictly serious suicidal motivation. However, the question then is raised of what one does with this information. The counselor perhaps should have dealt with this aspect directly by asking questions regarding what Jerry thought he might gain through this action. Of course, it can be argued that this line of confrontation might have only led the counselor to a dead end, with Jerry becoming more defensive and using more and more denial. While this is quite possible, the counselor must always assess whether or not the client is in a position to accept either a confrontation or an interpretation in the course of the interview.

When analyzing the consequences of Jerry's suicide gesture after the fact, the reader should know that he reestablished his relationship with Rhonda within a few days after he was seen. This probably comes as no surprise, for this is frequently the case. However, we have no way of knowing how long the relationship lasted after that nor the course it took. We can speculate that it quite probably had its dramatic ups and downs.

Another aspect to consider in this case is the dimension of Jerry's feelings of anger toward his girlfriend, his brother, his parents, some of his peers, and who knows how many others. It might have been quite appropriate for the counselor to look into this whole area of (1) how Jerry deals with anger, (2) what social channels are available to him to express anger, (3) what the consequences are, (4) what social and family support there is for such expression, and (5) how, and even if, Jerry recognizes that he might be in any way mad. We can speculate, based on what he says, that any assertive statements directed towards his parents are likely to arouse a certain amount of guilt in him. These and similar concerns could well have been dealt with even in the single interview. Then, depending upon the answers, the counselor might have been more effective in securing Jerry's cooperation in going along with a referral perhaps to the school counselor. Referring someone like this is always problematical. Sometimes the very least likely candidate will follow through, while the one adolescent that the counselor was sure would, never does.

Even in those cases in which it does not appear that the client will follow up, the counselor should in almost every case be prepared to offer a referral. There is always the possibility that something may change the client's mind at some later date, and if he has the referral information written down somewhere, he might just pick up on it and see it through. We always encourage the counselor to write down the name, address, and telephone number of the counselor or agency to whom he is referring the client, and to hand this information to the client. This adds weight to the referral, and we think it underscores the counselor's genuine concern that the client follow through.

While we have geared many of our comments in this case to work with males, we wish to emphasize that the same principles apply to female adolescents as well. In fact, in crisis work the counselor is much more likely to work with female suicide gesturers than males (Sarason 1972).

In crisis counseling with persons such as Jerry, one of the goals might have been for the counselor to work with him to help him express his frustration and anger in a more constructive way. Any time the counselor can help the client find more effective problem-solving measures that are less manipulative and less potentially self-destructive than a suicide gesture, the counselor should pursue them. This itself is frequently a difficult task and one that is often frustrating to the clinician.

In addition to helping the adolescent understand his or her behavior, there is the additional burden of trying to keep the adolescent in counseling. With so much change going on, it requires a considerable amount of skill to keep the adolescent client coming to his appointments.

With adolescents, or anyone else who is seen only once, making interpretations and engaging in confrontations can be, at best, a risky business. While it can be argued that someone in a state of crisis is more likely to be amenable to direct intervention, we think that in this case it is an "iffey" question. Other than the measures already suggested, there is little more that the counselor could have done. Those who have conducted any significant amount of crisis intervention may well tell you that there are likely to be numerous cases like Jerry's in which the best that the counselor can do is to hope to be there when the client makes the next maladaptive maneuver.

A few comments about the way the counselor handled the interview: For the most part, the counselor provided only as much structure as the client required. However, the counselor did as good a job as might be expected, given that most adolescents are fairly noncommunicative. She did make an attempt to deal with the client's anger, but simply did not pursue it far enough. On several occasions the counselor asked more than one question at a time, or asked closed-end questions. Furthermore, she brought the interview to a close too soon.

While this case was handled reasonably well, all things considered, there still remain some questions that the counselor should have had some answers to:

1. Did his parents have any inkling of this act? Did he tell them, or in some other way communicate to them his intentions? If they suspected, why didn't they say something?

2. Why didn't his brother say anything to the family? Is this typical of the family communication pattern? This leads one to consider that perhaps Jerry

had done this before, and as a result the family may have simply seen this as another of his childish behaviors. In this event they might not have become too upset by it.

3. Why did his brother treat this important event so lightly? Is this again some kind of family communication pattern, or has Jerry been manipulating everyone and simply manufacturing stories, selectively not telling everyone just exactly what has been going on?

Though we simply do not have answers to these questions, the crisis counselor, with experience, will learn to consider questions such as these when working with the adolescent in crisis.

Crisis counseling does not bring about significant or even minor change in every case. As mentioned at the beginning of the book, this approach has its limitations. Nevertheless, with a certain touch of reality the counselor will neither overlook the limits of this approach nor underestimate its potential as a sometimes viable alternative in the prevention of longer-standing chronic and maladaptive behavior patterns.

References

Haimowitz, M.L., and R.N. Haimowitz, eds. *Human Development: Selected Readings.* New York: Thomas Crowell Co., 1973.

Hofman, A.D., and R.D. Becker. "Psychotherapeutic Approaches to the Physically Ill Adolescent." *International Journal of Child Psychotherapy* 2 (1973): 492-511.

Sarason, I. *Abnormal Psychology.* New York: Appleton-Century-Croft, 1972.

Weinberg, S. "Suicidal Intent In Adolescence: A Hypothesis About The Role of Physical Illness." *Journal of Pediatrics* 77: 579-86.

Weiner, I. "Psychological Disturbance in Adolescence," *Interscience Series.* New York: John Wiley, 1970.

Barter, J.T., D. Swaback, and D. Todd. "Adolescent Suicide Attempts: A Follow Up Study of Hospitalized Patients." *Archives of General Psychiatry* 19 (1968): 523-27.

Additional Readings

Caplan, G., and S. Lebovici, eds. *Adolescence: Psychosocial Perspectives.* New York: Basic Books, 1969.

Erikson, E., ed. *Youth: Change and Challenge.* New York: Basic Books, 1963.

Erikson, E. *Identity: Youth and Crisis.* New York: W.W. Norton, 1968.

Josselyn, I. *The Adolescent and His World.* New York: Family Service Association of America, 1952.

Meeks, J.E. *The Fragile Alliance.* Baltimore: Williams & Wilkins, 1971.

Miller, D. *Adolescence: Psychology, Psychopathology and Psychotherapy.* New York: Jason Aronson, 1974.

Offer, D. *The Psychological World of the Teen-ager.* New York: Basic Books, 1969.

Usdin, G.L., ed. *Adolescence: Care and Counseling.* Philadelphia: J.B. Lippincott, 1967.

Appendixes

Appendix A:
The Social Readjustment
Rating Scale

Life Event	Mean Value
1. Death of spouse	100
2. Divorce	73
3. Marital separation	65
4. Jail term	63
5. Death of close family member	63
6. Personal injury or illness	53
7. Marriage	50
8. Fired at work	47
9. Marital reconciliation	45
10. Retirement	45
11. Change in health of family member	44
12. Pregnancy	40
13. Sex difficulties	39
14. Gain of new family member	39
15. Business readjustment	39
16. Change in financial state	38
17. Death of close friend	37
18. Change to different line of work	36
19. Change in number of arguments with spouse	35
20. Mortgage over $10,000	31
21. Foreclosure of mortgage or loan	30
22. Change in responsibilities at work	29
23. Son or daughter leaving home	29
24. Trouble with in-laws	29
25. Outstanding personal achievement	28
26. Wife begin or stop work	26
27. Begin or end school	26
28. Change in living conditions	25
29. Revision of personal habits	24
30. Trouble with boss	23
31. Change in work hours or conditions	20
32. Change in residence	20
33. Change in schools	20
34. Change in recreation	19
35. Change in church activities	19
36. Change in social activities	18
37. Mortgage or loan less than $10,000	17
38. Change in sleeping habits	16
39. Change in number of family get-togethers	15
40. Change in eating habits	15
41. Vacation	13
42. Christmas	12
43. Minor violations of the law	11

Source: T.H. Holmes and R.H. Rahe. "The Social Readjustment Rating Scale." *Journal of Psychosomatic Research* 213-218, 11 (1967): for complete wording of the items.

Appendix B:
Evaluation of Suicide
Risk

1. Marital Status. Divorced or separated people comprise a disproportionate percentage of suicides (Farberow et al. 1965) and widowed individuals show especially high rates (Sainsburg 1955). Their self-inflicted deaths cluster in the first years of bereavement (MacMahon et al. 1965).

The lowest rates appear to be among the married, especially those with children. The rates for single people average twice those of the married, and the rates for the divorced or widowed are from four to five times higher than the married (Hendin 1967).

2. Presence of Physical Illness. There is a high correlation between physical illness and suicidal behavior (Dorpat et al. 1968). The presence of a disabling or painful illness, such as cancer, particularly in someone who was robust, presents a considerable risk.

3. Depression. All patients whose mood is depressed should be carefully questioned as to their suicide potential (Susser 1968).

4. Severe Insomnia. Regular early morning wakening with restlessness indicates a high risk.

5. Correlation to Gender. The risk of suicide is higher among men (Susser 1968), although women may gesture more. Men will frequently make more lethal attempts using violent means, whereas women seem to prefer to overdose. The percentage of males and females are 70 and 30 respectively for successful suicides, while the percentage for attempted suicides are nearly the reverse, 31 and 69 respectively (Farberow and Shneidman 1965).

6. Schizophrenia. Clinical experience suggests that suicidal behavior is much more difficult to predict in schizophrenics (Farberow and Shneidman 1957). A combination of a depressed mood, a thought disorder, and suicidal ideation is ominous. Especially ominous are "command" hallucinations telling the patient to kill himself, or the hallucination of the voice of a departed loved one beckoning the patient to join him in the world beyond.

7. Alcoholism and Drug Addiction. Clinical experience shows that suicidal behavior is difficult to predict in alcoholics (Farberow and Shneidman 1957) and in drug addicts. While an addict or alcoholic may not consciously elect to kill himself, his judgment may become impaired to the point where he might, for instance, take an excess of barbiturates in order to sleep. In susceptible individuals alcohol or drugs can also trigger violence aimed at oneself or at others. Alcoholism or drug addiction may, in addition, be an expression of an underlying neurosis or psychosis; these disorders may of themselves increase the

Reprinted with the permission of the authors and Harper & Row from J. Lieb, Ian Lipsitch and Andrew Slaby, *The Crisis Team* (New York: Harper & Row, 1973), pp. 61-64.

risk of suicide. It is believed by some that any addiction, because of the incredible toll it takes on the individual both physically and emotionally, represents a form of chronic suicidal behavior.

8. Homosexuality. Homosexuals, particularly those inclined to alcoholism and depression, and those who entertain florid sadomasochistic fantasies, should be carefully assessed for suicidal potential. The aging homosexual whose physical attractiveness is declining constitutes a serious risk. Society still continues to treat homosexuals as outcasts, thus engendering situations where homosexuals are prevented from moving within the mainstream and have to depend for support on the homosexual subculture. The homosexual subculture does not, by and large, attract persons who are noted for their emotional stability, and so a vicious circle is established in which many homosexuals are denied exposure to stable supports. According to Socarides (1968), approximately one-half of individuals who engage in homosexual practices have concomitant schizophrenia, paranoia, are latent or pseudoneurotic schizophrenics, or are in the throes of a manic-depressive reaction. The other half, *when neurotic*, may be character disorders or addicts. Bieber et al. (1965), in reporting on over one hundred homosexuals who sought treatment, stated that one-third are character disorders. While homosexuality does not necessarily denote psychopathology, it is clear that there is a high correlation and the risk of suicide is compounded.

9. Previous Suicide Attempts. Studies have shown that 50-80 percent of those who commit suicide have a history of a previous suicide attempt (Susser 1968).

10. Lethality of Attempt. Shneidman and Farberow (1965) divide suicides into two groups: those in which the point of no return is rapidly reached and those in which it is gradually reached. Gunshot wounds, hanging, and jumping, which are associated with a quick death, are identified almost entirely with lethal attempts, whereas wrist cutting, throat cutting, and ingestions are associated with nonfatal attempts. The more violent and painful the method chosen, the greater the risk.

The setting in which the attempt occurs (e.g., is there likelihood of immediate discovery?) and whether an attempt is made to communicate to others are important considerations. Suicidal ideas harbored by the patient and not communicated to his relatives constitute a grave situation. A suicide attempt is more serious when a note has been written. Szasz (1959) believes that suicidal behavior may constitute a form of communication, or as Shneidman and Farberow prefer, "a cry for help." A suicide attempt is less malignant when it can be determined that secondary gain is involved.

11. Living Arrangements. Suicide risk is greater among those who live alone (Susser 1968; McMahon et al. 1963).

12. Age. Advancing age and suicide rates are directly correlated. Suicides are virtually nonexistent before nine years of age and rare in the ten-to-fourteen-year-old age group (less than one death for 200,000 children). However, the

rate rises sharply from age fifteen to nineteen (an eight-to-tenfold increase); from age twenty to twenty-four the suicide rate doubles again. This trend continues to the very old adult (Shneidman and Farberow 1957).

13. Religion. Jews and Catholics seem to have lower suicide rates than Protestants (Durkheim 1897).

14. Race. It appears that proportionately more blacks attempt suicide than commit it. Shneidman and Farberow report that 95 percent of successful suicides in their group were white. Certain subgroups are atypical; while suicide among urban black males aged twenty to thirty-five is nearly twice that for white men of a comparable age group, in older age groups the white suicide is significantly higher (Hendin 1967).

15. Family History of Suicide. A history of suicide in the family must be asked about. In one series, 25 percent of those who attempted suicide had a history of suicide in the immediate family (Shneidman and Farberow 1957).

16. Recent Loss. The recent loss through death of a person close to the patient has also been found to be a precipitating factor in suicide (Shneidman and Farberow 1957).

Other factors cited as increasing the risk of suicide include hypochondriasis, recent surgery or childbirth, no apparent secondary gain, unemployment, and financial difficulty.

In evaluating a patient who has attempted suicide or is contemplating it, it is crucial to assess how depressed the patient is and to inquire specifically about guilt feelings, self-depreciation, or nihilistic ideas. The patient who persistently claims that he or others would be better off if he were dead constitutes a serious risk.

References

Bieber, I. *Homosexuality*. New York: Vintage, 1965.

Dorpat, T.L., W.F. Anderson, and H.S. Ripley. "The Relationship of Physical Illness to Suicide." In *Suicidal Behaviors* (Ed. H.L.P. Resnik). Boston: Little, Brown, 1968.

Durkheim, E. *Le Suicide: Étude de Sociologie* (Suicide: A Study in Sociology). Paris: Alcan, 1897.

Farberow, N.L., and E.S. Shneidman, eds. *The Cry for Help*. New York: McGraw-Hill, 1965.

Hendin, H. "Suicide." In *Comprehensive Textbook of Psychiatry* (Ed. A.M. Freedman and H.I. Kaplan) Baltimore: Williams and Wilkins, 1967.

MacMahon, B., S. Johnson, and T.F. Pugh. "Relation of Suicide Rates to Social Conditions." *Public Health Report* 78 (1963): 285-93.

MacMahon, B., and T.F. Pugh. "Suicide in the Widowed." *American Journal of Epidemiology* 81 (1965): 23-31.

Sainsburg, P. *Suicide in London*. London: Chapman and Hall, 1955.

Shneidman, E.S., and N.L. Farberow. *Clues to Suicide*. New York: McGraw-Hill, 1957.

Socarides, C.W. *The Overt Homosexual*. New York: Grune and Stratton, 1968.

Susser, M. *Community Psychiatry, Epidemiologic and Social Theories*. New York: Random House, 1968.

Szasz, T.S. "The Communication of Distress between Child and Parent." *British Journal of Medical Psychiatry* 32 (1959): 161-70.

Appendix C:
Mental Status Examination
Record (MSER)

Form MS9 (9/70)

MENTAL STATUS EXAMINATION RECORD (MSER)*   Read instructions on reverse side.   Page 1 of 4

Patient's last name	First name	M.I.	Facility	Ward

IDENTIFICATION

:0:: :1:: :2:: :3:: :4::   :5:: :6:: :7:: :8:: :9::

Case or consecutive number

:0:: :1:: :2:: :3:: :4::   :5:: :6:: :7:: :8:: :9::

:0:: :1:: :2:: :3:: :4::   :5:: :6:: :7:: :8:: :9::

:0:: :1:: :2:: :3:: :4::   :5:: :6:: :7:: :8:: :9::

:0:: :1:: :2:: :3:: :4::   :5:: :6:: :7:: :8:: :9::

Facility code

:0:: :1:: :2:: :3:: :4::   :5:: :6:: :7:: :8:: :9::

:0:: :1:: :2:: :3:: :4::   :5:: :6:: :7:: :8:: :9::

:0:: :1:: :2:: :3:: :4::   :5:: :6:: :7:: :8:: :9::

Rater code

:0:: :1:: :2:: :3:: :4::   :5:: :6:: :7:: :8:: :9::

:0:: :1:: :2:: :3:: :4::   :5:: :6:: :7:: :8:: :9::

:0:: :1:: :2:: :3:: :4::   :5:: :6:: :7:: :8:: :9::

Last day of week being evaluated

Jan	Feb	Mar	Apr	May	Month	Jun	Jul	Aug	Sep	Oct
1	69	70	71	72	Year	73	74	75	Nov	Dec
2	3	4	5	6		7	8	9	10	11
12	13	14	15	16	Day	17	18	19	20	21
22	23	24	25	26		27	28	29	30	31

Sex of the patient

male   female

Patient's age

:0:: :1:: :2:: :3:: :4::   :5:: :6:: :7:: :8:: :9::

:0:: :1:: :2:: :3:: :4::   :5:: :6:: :7:: :8:: :9::

TRANSACTION

initial evaluation   reeval-uation   partial reeval   correc-tion   dele-tion

ATTITUDE TOWARD RATER

unknown

very positive | positive | neutral | ambivalent | negative | very negative

RELIABILITY AND COMPLETENESS OF INFORMATION

very good | good | only fair | poor | very poor

quality of speech

Barriers to communication or reliability were due to

refuses information	massive denial	dialect or foreign language
physical illness	preoccupation	lack of response
sensorial or cognitive disorder	conscious falsification	deafness

APPEARANCE

Patient looks   his age | older | younger | good looking

Apparent physical health   very good | good | only fair | poor | very poor

Physical deformity   slight | mild | mod | mark

Weight   underweight | average | overweight   gain-ing | los-ing

Height   very short | short | average | tall | very tall

Ambulation disturbance   walks with assistance | must use wheel chair | bed-ridden

Dress and grooming

	slight	mild	mod	mark
Unkempt	:2:	:3:	:4:	:5:
Inappropriate	:2:	:3:	:4:	:5:
Seductive	:2:	:3:	:4:	:5:
Neat and appropriate for occasion				

Posture

	slight	mild	mod	mark
Stooped	:2:	:3:	:4:	:5:
Stiff	:2:	:3:	:4:	:5:
Bizarre	:2:	:3:	:4:	:5:

Face

Impassive		:2:	:4:	:5:
Tense	:2:	:3:	:4:	:5:
Perplexed	:2:	:3:	:4:	:5:
Suspicious	:2:	:3:	:4:	:5:
Angry	:2:	:3:	:4:	:5:
Sullen	:2:	:3:	:4:	:5:
Bored	:2:	:3:	:4:	:5:
Worried	:2:	:3:	:4:	:5:
Sad	:2:	:3:	:4:	:5:
Tearful	:2:	:3:	:4:	:5:
Elated	:2:	:3:	:4:	:5:
Silly	:2:	:3:	:4:	:5:
Grimacing	:2:	:3:	:4:	:5:
Hypervigilant	:2:	:3:	:4:	:5:
Facial expression unremarkable				

Eyes

	occa-sional	often	very often	most of time
Avoids direct gaze				
Stares into space				
Glances furtively				

Set no. 0056488   Mark last 3 digits of Set number in area below.

:0:: :1:: :2:: :3:: :4::   :5:: :6:: :7:: :8:: :9::

:0:: :1:: :2:: :3:: :4::   :5:: :6:: :7:: :8:: :9::

*Developed by Robert L. Spitzer, M.D., and Jean Endicott, Ph.D., Biometrics Research, N.Y.S. Department of Mental Hygiene, with the assistance of the Multi-State Information System for Psychiatric Patients Project. Supported by N.Y.S. Department of Mental Hygiene, C29820 and NIMH Grants 14934 and 08534.

MSER 1b

PURPOSE

The purpose of the Mental Status Examination Record (MSER) is to enable a rater to record the results of a mental status examination. Proper use of this form encourages the rater to consider all of the items on the MSER when conducting his examination. The recorded information can be used by a computer to produce a narrative description of the results of the examination. In addition, it will also be possible to use the information for the systematic evaluation of individual patients and for studies of groups of patients.

The rater may add narrative comments to the clinical record for any information for which there are no items on the form.

DATA SOURCE

The data upon which the judgments are based should be mainly from direct contact with the patient; however, other information available to the rater, such as nurses' reports or personal observation of the patient on the ward, should be used.

TIME PERIOD

The evaluation covers behavior and symptoms which occurred during the week prior to and including the day of evaluation whether the evaluation is done on admission or at a later time.

ITEMS OF INFORMATION

Some items must be marked for all patients. These items are printed in **bold type** and contain a category indicating no pathology. For example:

Psychomotor none slight mild mod mark
retardation ::1:: ::2:: ::3:: ::4:: ::5::

All of the remaining items are marked only when applicable for the patient being evaluated. These items should be left blank if there is no information or if there is no psychopathology. Examples are:

sus-
pected slight mild mod mark
Drug abuse ::::: ::2:: ::3:: ::4:: ::5::

hallucinogen   barbiturate
:::::   :::::

Note that a shaded line, linking a series of terms in an item requiring a scaled judgment, indicates that the rater should select no more than one term from the list.

All scaled judgments of severity should take into account how intense the behavior was as well as how much of the time it was present during the week. Thus, the ratings are a weighted average for the entire week and not necessarily the highest intensity exhibited at any one time. When making these judgments, the rater should think of the full range of the behavior that people sometimes exhibit.

NOTING JUDGMENTS

Note all judgments with a No. 2 pencil. Make a heavy dark mark between the lines of the grids. Example ▬ To change a judgment, completely erase the incorrect mark. In filling out **IDENTIFICATION** section and **Set number,** numbers should be written in the boxes as well as noted in the grids. The numbers read from top to bottom so that the last digit is in the bottom row. If the number has fewer digits than the number of rows alloted, one or more of the top rows are left blank.

SET NUMBER

Each page of the MSER is preprinted with a seven digit Set number. The last three digits of this number are used to link the four pages together for data processing. Be sure to mark the last three digits from the Set number on all four pages.

PRINTOUT

The computer printout will contain in a narrative all of the information that the rater has noted. This will include information based on ratings of "none" as well as positive indications of psychopathology.

If a rater fails to mark an item that is supposed to be completed for all patients, the printout will note that information for this item is missing. Inconsistencies between ratings will also be indicated.

IBM M62390

DEFINITIONS AND INSTRUCTIONS for sections and items which may be unclear.

IDENTIFICATION

Rater code Code number for person completing this form.

Last day of week being evaluated The last day of the one week being evaluated. Not necessarily the same as date the form is completed.

TRANSACTION

Initial evaluation for first time entire form used for this admission.
Reevaluation for subsequent use of entire form.
Partial reevaluation Entry of IDENTIFICATION and one or more sections of the form to indicate a change in patient's condition since the last entry. The printout will be limited to those sections.
Correction To make a correction in a previously submitted form, because of clerical or judgmental error, or new information, correct old form or completely fill out a new form. The case or consecutive number and date in the IDENTIFICATION section must be identical to the previously submitted form. The previously submitted form will be completely replaced in the file by the new form.
Deletion To delete from the file a previously submitted form, e.g. wrong case or consecutive number, wrong date, or duplicate record. Form requesting deletion must have identical case or consecutive number and date in IDENTIFICATION section as record to be deleted.

ATTITUDE TOWARD RATER

Unknown as might be the case with a mute patient.
Ambivalent At times positive, at other times, negative.
Neutral No particular emotional reaction.

RELIABILITY AND COMPLETENESS OF INFORMATION

Rater's overall judgment of accuracy and completeness of information. Example: a mute catatonic would not give information about the content of his thoughts, thereby lowering the completeness of the overall information.
Barriers to communication or reliability were due to the specific reason(s) listed.

Quality of speech Any disturbance of speech listed later under "Quality of speech and thought" which is a barrier to communication.
Preoccupation Exclusive focus on a topic or thought so that inadequate information is given on other topics.
Massive denial Extensive use of the defense mechanism of denial where aspects of external reality are not acknowledged so as to avoid anxiety, as distinguished from lying which is conscious.
Lack of response Failure to reply to questions.
Sensorial or cognitive disorder Any disturbance listed under "Sensorium" or "Cognitive functions" which is a barrier to communication.

APPEARANCE

Apparent physical health Outward appearance of health.
Physical deformity Visibility of physical deformity causing disfigurement.
Dress and grooming Clothing, hair, makeup, jewelry, accessories.
    Unkempt Untidy or dirty.
    Inappropriate Odd or eccentric or unsuitable for the occasion.
Posture
    Stiff Holding body rigidly.
    Bizarre Odd or eccentric.
Face Facial expression. It need not be consistent with "General attitude and behavior," as with a patient who looks angry but does not act angry.
    Impassive Expressionless. When marked may be like a "zombie."
    Grimacing Distorted facial expression.
    Hypervigilant Excessive watchfulness and attentiveness, as staring closely at interviewer.
Eyes
    Glances furtively Looks about quickly and surreptitiously.

Form MS9 (9/70)
MSER

MOTOR BEHAVIOR

		none	slight	mild	mod	marked
Psychomotor retardation		::1::	::2::	::3::	::4::	::5::
catatonic stupor		catatonic rigidity				waxy flexibility

		none	slight	mild	mod	marked
Psychomotor excitement		::1::	::2::	::3::	::4::	::5::
		catatonic excitement				

		slight	mild	mod	marked
Tremor		::2::	::3::	::4::	::5::
Tics		::2::	::3::	::4::	::5::
Posturing		::2::	::3::	::4::	::5::
Pacing		::2::	::3::	::4::	::5::
Fidgeting		::2::	::3::	::4::	::5::
Gait	Unsteadiness	::2::	::3::	::4::	::5::
	Rigidity	::2::	::3::	::4::	::5::
	Slowness	::2::	::3::	::4::	::5::

Motor abnormality possibly because of

	orthopedic problem	neurological disorder
medication	::::::	::::::

GENERAL ATTITUDE AND BEHAVIOR

Positive characteristics

		good sense of humor
helpful	responsible	::::::
cheerful	pleasant	likeable

	none	slight	mild	mod	marked
Uncooperative	::1::	::2::	::3::	::4::	::5::
Withdrawn	::1::	::2::	::3::	::4::	::5::
Inappropriate	::1::	::2::	::3::	::4::	::5::
Impaired functioning in goal directed activities	::1::	::2::	::3::	::4::	::5::
Suspicious	::1::	::2::	::3::	::4::	::5::
Anger (overt)	::1::	::2::	::3::	::4::	::5::

sarcastic	critical	argumentative
sullen	assaultive	physically destructive
irritable	threatens violence	

		slight	mild	mod	marked
Provokes anger		::2::	::3::	::4::	::5::

	none	at least threats	at least gesture(s)	attempt(s)
Suicidal behavior	::::::	::::::	::::::	::::::

	slight	mild	mod	marked
Self mutilation (degree of disfiguring)	::2::	::3::	::4::	::5::
Antisocial	::2::	::3::	::4::	::5::
Impulsive	::2::	::3::	::4::	::5::
Passive	::2::	::3::	::4::	::5::
Dependent	::2::	::3::	::4::	::5::
Domineering	::2::	::3::	::4::	::5::
Guarded	::2::	::3::	::4::	::5::
Complaining	::2::	::3::	::4::	::5::
Ritualistic	::2::	::3::	::4::	::5::

GENERAL ATTITUDE AND BEHAVIOR (continued)

		slight	mild	mod	mark
Obsequious		::2::	::3::	::4::	::5::
Despondent		::2::	::3::	::4::	::5::
Apathetic		::2::	::3::	::4::	::5::
Fearful		::2::	::3::	::4::	::5::
Dramatic		::2::	::3::	::4::	::5::
Sexually seductive		::2::	::3::	::4::	::5::
Homosexual behavior		::2::	::3::	::4::	::5::
Alcohol abuse	suspected ::::::	::2::	::3::	::4::	::5::
Drug abuse	suspected ::::::	::2::	::3::	::4::	::5::
hallucinogen	barbiturate				stimulant
::::::	::::::				
narcotic	other				
::::::	::::::				

MOOD AND AFFECT

	none	slight	mild	mod	mark
Depression	::1::	::2::	::3::	::4::	::5::
Anxiety	::1::	::2::	::3::	::4::	::5::
	with episodes of panic ::::::				
Anger	::1::	::2::	::3::	::4::	::5::
Euphoria		::2::	::3::	::4::	::5::
Anhedonia		::2::	::3::	::4::	::5::
Loneliness		::2::	::3::	::4::	::5::

Quality of mood and affect

	none	slight	mild	mod	mark
Flatness	::1::	::2::	::3::	::4::	::5::
Inappropriate	::1::	::2::	::3::	::4::	::5::
Lability	::1::	::2::	::3::	::4::	::5::
Diurnal mood variation		::2::		::4::	::5::
	worse in morning ::::::				worse in evening

QUALITY OF SPEECH AND THOUGHT

Voice	shouts ::::::		screams ::::::
very loud ::::::	monotonous ::::::		overly dramatic ::::::
whining ::::::	very soft ::::::		

	very slow	slow	average	fast	very fast
Rate	::::::	::::::	::::::	::::::	::::::

	markedly reduced	reduced	average	increased	markedly increased
Productivity	::::::	::::::	::::::	::::::	::::::

	none	slight	mild	mod	mark
Incoherence	::1::	::2::	::3::	::4::	::5::
Irrelevance	::1::	::2::	::3::	::4::	::5::
Evasiveness	::1::	::2::	::3::	::4::	::5::
Blocking		::2::	::3::	::4::	::5::

Set no. 0056488

Mark last 3 digits of Set number in area below.

::0::	::1::	::2::	::3::	::4::					
::0::	::1::	::2::	::3::	::4::	::5::	::6::	::7::	::8::	::9::
::0::	::1::	::2::	::3::	::4::	::5::	::6::	::7::	::8::	::9::

IBM M62391

MOTOR BEHAVIOR

Characteristics of bodily movements that are observable.
Psychomotor retardation Generalized slowing down of physical reactions and movements.

Catatonic stupor Marked decrease in reactivity to environment and reduction of spontaneous movements and activity. May appear to be unaware of nature of surroundings.

Catatonic rigidity Maintaining a rigid posture against efforts to move him.

Waxy flexibility Maintaining postures into which he is placed.

Psychomotor excitement Generalized overactivity.

Catatonic excitement Apparently purposeless and stereotyped, excited motor activity not influenced by external stimuli.

Tics Involuntary, brief, recurrent, movements involving a relatively small segment of the body.

Posturing Voluntary assumption of an inappropriate or bizarre posture.

GENERAL ATTITUDE AND BEHAVIOR

The attitude and behavior that the patient displays in his inter-action with others. This may or may not be consistent with "Content of speech and thought." For example: he may be physically assaultive but not indicate or acknowledge thoughts of doing violence to others.

Withdrawn Avoidance of contact or involvement with people.

Inappropriate Behavior that is odd, eccentric or not in keeping with the situation. Examples: exposing self, talking to self, frequent giggling.

Impaired functioning in goal directed activities Impairment in work (if work was expected) or in other goal directed activities, e.g. chores, leisure time activities, or getting dressed.

Suspicious From mild distrust to feelings of persecution. May be markedly suspicious and yet not delusional.

Anger (overt) Overall rating of overt expression of anger. In-ferences of unconscious anger should not be used in making this rating.

Assaultive Physical violence against a person.

Physically destructive Destroys or breaks things.

Provokes anger Attitude or behavior that provokes anger in others, e.g. teases, touches others, argumentative.

Suicidal behavior As distinguished from suicidal thoughts. In-clude evaluation of threat to life and seriousness of intent.

Self mutilation Disfigurement resulting from deliberate damage to the body (not associated with a suicide attempt).

Antisocial Antisocial attitude or behavior, e.g. lying, encourag-ing breaking of rules, stealing, complacent attitude towards his own or others' antisocial behavior.

Impulsive Acts immediately without reflection.

Passive Permits himself to be acted upon without his making efforts to control the course of events.

Dependent Seeks undue assistance, praise or reassurance from others.

Domineering Examples: tries to control interview, orders others around.

Guarded Acts in a defensive or protective manner, e.g. reluctant to give information.

Ritualistic Displays compulsions or other repetitive stereo-typed behavior that is not directly adaptive, e.g. hand washing rituals, endless recheckings, formalized procedures for eating or dressing.

Obsequious Servile attentiveness or marked inclination to please.

Despondent Acts discouraged, dejected, or depressed.

Apathetic Lack of feeling, interest, concern or emotion.

Dramatic Artificiality of action with exaggerated emotionalism.

Homosexual behavior Overt homosexual approaches or acts as distinguished from homosexual thoughts.

Alcohol abuse Use of alcohol during the past week which is ex-cessive, causes physical symptoms, causes alteration in mood or behavior, or interferes with performance of expected daily routine or duties.

Drug abuse Excessive self medication; unprescribed use of drugs with effects as described above for alcohol abuse.

MOOD AND AFFECT

Emotion or feeling tone that is either observable or reported by the patient. This may or may not be consistent with the content of speech, e.g. looks sad and tearful but says he is not depressed. Inferences based on psychodynamic formulations should not be used in making these ratings, e.g. unconscious anger because the patient is overly polite.

Depression Sadness, worthlessness, failure, hopelessness, re-morse, or loss.

Anxiety Apprehension, worry, nervousness, tension, fearfulness, or panic.

With episodes of panic Circumscribed periods of intense anxiety.

Euphoria Exaggerated feeling of well being, not consonant with circumstances.

Anhedonia Absence of pleasure in activities that ordinarily would be pleasurable.

Flatness Generalized impoverishment of emotional reactivity, often described as "emotionally dull," or "unresponsive."

Inappropriate Affect is not appropriate for situation or is in-congruous with content of speech, e.g. giggles during interview, cheerful while discussing threats to his life.

Lability Unstable emotions that shift rapidly without adequate control, e.g. sudden bursts of anger or crying.

Diurnal mood variation Consistent change in mood from morning to evening.

QUALITY OF SPEECH AND THOUGHT

Voice monotonous Lack of normal variation in pitch.

Rate Rapidity of speech and thought.

Productivity The amount of speech.

Incoherence Impairment in the form of speech which makes it difficult to understand or follow. (A bizarre delusional belief may be explained in a coherent manner.)

Irrelevance Content of remarks is not related to questions being asked or topic under discussion.

Evasiveness Deliberately avoids answering questions directly.

Blocking Sudden cessation in the train of thought or in the middle of a sentence. The patient is unable to explain the reason for the sudden stoppage.

Form MS 9 (9/70)

MSER

QUALITY OF SPEECH AND THOUGHT (continued)

	slight	mild	mod	marked
Circumstantiality				
Loosening of associations				
Obscurity				
Concreteness				

Other

echolalia	clang associations		neologisms
flight of ideas	excessive profanity		plays on words
persever-ation	unintelligible muttering		suggestive of neurological disorder

CONTENT OF SPEECH AND THOUGHT

	unknown	none	slight	mild	mod	marked
Grandiosity						
Suicidal ideation						
Ideas of reference						
Bizarre thoughts						
Phobia(s)						
Compulsion(s)						
Obsession(s)						
Guilt						
Alienation						
Pessimism						
Distrustfulness						
Self pity						
Inadequacy						
Diminished interest						
Indecisiveness						
Isolation						
Helplessness						
Failure						
Loss						
Self derogatory						
Resentful of others						
Death						
Loss of control						

Harm	being harmed by others	doing harm to others
Sexual symptoms	frigidity	homosexual impulses
	potency disturbance	fears of homosexuality

Delusions	absent	unknown	suspected	likely	definite

	slight	mild	mod	marked
Persecutory delusions				
Somatic delusions				
Delusions of grandeur				

CONTENT OF SPEECH AND THOUGHT (continued)

	slight	mild	mod	mark
Religious delusions				
Delusions of guilt				
Delusions of influence				
Nihilistic delusions				

Influence of delusion on behavior	very little	considerable	marked

SOMATIC FUNCTIONING AND CONCERN

Appetite	very poor	poor	normal	excessive	very excessive
		requires urging to eat		requires help to eat	

Energy level	very easily fatigued	easily fatigued	normal	very energetic	extremely energetic
	sleeps excessively			feels little need for sleep	

Change in sexual interest or activity	marked decrease	slight decrease	slight increase	marked increase

Insomnia (overall severity any type)	none	slight	mild	mod	mark
difficulty falling asleep	early morning awakening		awakening during night		

Incontinence	occa-sionally	often	very often	most of time

Seizures (this week)	one	several	daily	several per day
	likely hysterical		likely organic	

Severe sensory impairment (organic)	visual	hearing

Conversion reaction	suspected	likely	definite
Type	hearing loss		visual defect
paralysis	anesthesia		paresthesia
abnormal movements	pain		

Psychophysiologic reactions	none	slight	mild	mod	mark
Type	upset stomach		diarrhea		
consti-pation	palpitations		hyperventilation syndrome		
headache	back-ache		urinary frequency		
sweating	itching				

Unwarranted concern with physical health	none	slight	mild	mod	mark

PERCEPTION

Hallucinations	absent	unknown	suspected	likely	definite

	slight	mild	mod	marked	un-formed	formed
Visual						
Auditory					voices	noises
Olfactory						
Gustatory						
Tactile						
Visceral						

Set no. **0056488**

Mark last 3 digits of Set number in area below.

:0:	:1:	:2:	:3:	:4:		:5:	:6:	:7:	:8:	:9:
:0:	:1:	:2:	:3:	:4:		:5:	:6:	:7:	:8:	:9:
:0:	:1:	:2:	:3:	:4:		:5:	:6:	:7:	:8:	:9:

IBM M62393

MSER 3b

Circumstantiality Proceeding indirectly to goal idea with many tedious details and parenthetical and irrelevant additions.
Loosening of associations Saying things in juxtaposition which lack a logical or inherent relationship, e.g. "I'm tired. All people have eyes."
Obscurity Lack of precision and clarity.
Concreteness A tendency to deal with concepts at a sensory or partial level at the expense of considering general relationships or abstractions, e.g. literal interpretation of proverbs.
Echolalia Repetition by imitation of phrases or words said in their presence.
Clang associations Combining unrelated words or phrases because they share similar sounds, e.g. "I'm sad, mad, bad."
Neologisms Invention of new words.
Flight of ideas Abrupt and rapid changes of topic of conversation so that ideas are not completed.
Plays on words Inappropriate rhyming or punning.
Perseveration Repetition of a single response or idea in reply to various questions or repetition of words or phrases over and over in a mechanical manner.
Suggestive of neurological disorder Impairment in articulation such as those seen in various neurological disorders or expressive aphasia.

CONTENT OF SPEECH AND THOUGHT
The items in this section are descriptive of what the patient says or is thinking about. It may not be in keeping with his attitude and general behavior. For example, he may not act "dependent" yet reports feelings of "helplessness." The information may be offered spontaneously or only after questioning.
Grandiosity Inflated appraisal of his worth, contact, power or knowledge. (A patient may be markedly grandiose and yet not have delusions of grandeur.)
Suicidal ideation From occasional thoughts of killing himself, to preoccupation with method of killing himself.
Ideas of reference Detection of personal reference in seemingly insignificant remarks, objects, or events, e.g. interprets a person's sneeze as a message. (Patient may recognize absurdity of thought.)
Bizarre thoughts Content of thinking is odd, eccentric or unusual (but not necessarily delusional), e.g. preoccupation with flying saucers.
Phobia Irrational fear of a specific object or situation, e.g. fear of crowds, heights, animals; to be distinguished from free floating anxiety or fears of general conditions (getting sick, business failure).
Compulsion An insistent, repetitive, unwanted urge to perform an act which is contrary to his ordinary conscious wishes or standards, e.g. hand washing compulsion.
Obsession Persistent, unwanted thoughts which occur against his resistance, the content of which he regards as senseless, e.g. thoughts of killing child.
Alienation Feelings of estrangement, e.g. wonders who he really is, feels he is different from everybody.
Isolation Feelings of social isolation, rejection, or discomfort with people; preference for being alone.
Loss Feelings or theme of no longer having some person or object of great importance.
Self derogatory Reproaches self for things he has done or not done.
Being harmed by others Thinks of people as mistreating him, as taking advantage of him or as harming him in some way.
Frigidity Impaired pleasure from sexual intercourse.
Fears of homosexuality Fears of homosexual seduction or fears that he is a homosexual.
Potency disturbance Difficulty maintaining an erection during intercourse.
Homosexual impulses Speaks of his homosexual impulses.
Delusions Conviction in some important personal belief which is almost certainly not true.
    Persecutory delusions Examples: believes an organized conspiracy exists against him, or that he has been attacked, harassed, cheated or persecuted or that people talk about him or stare at him, when the circumstances make it almost certainly not true.
    Somatic delusions Conviction about his body that is almost certainly not true, e.g. body is rotting, someone is in his brain.

Delusions of grandeur Claims power or knowledge beyond the bounds of credibility, e.g. has special relation to God; can read people's minds.
Religious delusions A delusion involving a religious theme.
Delusions of guilt Belief that he has done something terrible or is responsible for some event or condition which is almost certainly not true, e.g. has ruined family by his bad thoughts.
Delusions of influence Claims his thoughts, mood, or actions are controlled or mysteriously influenced by other people or by strange forces.
Nihilistic delusions Believes the world is destroyed or that he or everyone is dead.
Influence of delusion on behavior The extent to which the delusional belief influences his behavior. To be left blank if patient is not delusional or if his delusion has virtually no effect on how he interacts with others or how he organizes his life.

SOMATIC FUNCTIONING AND CONCERN
Energy Level Capacity to sustain effort without fatigue. The effort may not be goal directed as with the extremely energetic manic.
Change in sexual interest or activity To be left blank if there is no change from the usual level.
Insomnia Overall rating of difficulty sleeping.
Incontinence Inability to restrain, within normal limits, the natural evacuation of the bladder or bowels.
Seizures A sudden attack of motor or sensory disturbance often involving a disturbance of consciousness.
    Likely hysterical Judged to be on a psychological basis.
    Likely organic Judged to be due to some structural or biochemical abnormality of the brain.
Severe sensory impairment (organic) Examples: blindness, deafness on a physical basis.
Conversion reaction A disturbance of the special senses or of the voluntary nervous system, often expressing emotional conflict in a symbolic manner; to be distinguished from psychophysiologic disorders which are mediated by the autonomic nervous system, from malingering which is done consciously, and from neurological lesions which cause anatomically circumscribed symptoms. Symptoms should not be listed unless they are considered conversion reactions. ("Hysterical hallucinations" should not be noted here but rather under "Perception.")
    Anesthesia Absence of sensation, generally of the skin.
    Paresthesia Perverted sense of touch, e.g. tingling, burning, tickling caused by tactile stimulus.
    Abnormal movements Examples: tremors, tics, seizures, ataxic gait.
Psychophysiologic reactions Physical symptoms usually mediated by the autonomic nervous system, and clearly caused by emotional factors. The physiological changes are those that normally accompany certain emotional states, are generally reversible and therefore do not involve permanent tissue alteration.
    Upset stomach Do not include diarrhea or constipation even if the subject refers to these symptoms as "upset stomach."
    Hyperventilation syndrome Overbreathing which may cause such symptoms as breathlessness, dizziness, paresthesias and feelings of pressure in the chest.
Unwarranted concern with physical health Concern with physical health that is apparently not warranted by actual physical condition. Include concern with one organ (e.g. cardiac neurosis) as well as with multiple organs (hypochondriasis).

PERCEPTION
Hallucinations Sensory perceptions in the absence of identifiable stimulation occurring during the waking state whether judged to be on an organic, functional, psychotic, or hysterical basis.
    Visual hallucinations
    Unformed Visual hallucinations of unformed lights, flashes, or patterns.
    Formed Visual hallucinations of people, animals, or other recognizable things.
    Auditory hallucinations Hallucinations of sounds.
    Olfactory hallucinations Hallucinations of smell.
    Gustatory hallucinations Hallucinations of taste.
    Tactile hallucinations Hallucinations of touch.
    Visceral hallucinations Hallucinations of sensations arising within the body.

Form MS 9 (9/70)

MSER

PERCEPTION (continued)

Content of hallucinations

threatening	accusatory	flattering
benign	religious	self derogatory
grandiose	reassuring	sexual

Conviction hallucinations real — knows unreal / unsure / convinced

Illusions — slight mild mod marked

Depersonalization

Derealization

Deja vu

SENSORIUM

Orientation disturbance — too disturbed to test

Time — unknown none slight mild mod marked

Place

Person (self and others)

Memory disturbance — too disturbed to test / confabulation

Recent — unknown none slight mild mod marked

Remote

Clouding of consciousness — fluctuating / continuous

Dissociation

| trance | amnesia | fugue |
| hysterical attack | other | |

COGNITIVE FUNCTIONS

Attention disturbance — slight mild mod marked

Distractability

Intelligence (estimate) — unknown superior bright average borderline retarded

JUDGMENT

	very good	good	only fair	poor	very poor
Family relations					
Other social relations	very good	good	only fair	poor	very poor
Employment	very good	good	only fair	poor	very poor
Future plans	no plans (or) very good	good	only fair	poor	very poor

POTENTIAL FOR SUICIDE OR VIOLENCE

Suicide — unsure not significant low mod high very high

Physical violence — unsure not significant low mod high very high

INSIGHT AND ATTITUDE TOWARD ILLNESS

Recognition that he is ill — not applicable unknown

very good / good / only fair / little / none | says physically ill only

INSIGHT AND ATTITUDE TOWARD ILLNESS (continued)

Motivation for working on problem — not applicable unknown

very good / good / only fair / little / none | desires refuses treatment offered

Awareness of his contribution to difficulties — not applicable unknown

very good / good / only fair / little / none | blames circumstances others

OVERALL SEVERITY OF ILLNESS

not ill slight mild mod marked severe among most extreme

CHANGE IN CONDITION DURING PAST WEEK

marked improv / impr / stable / variable / worse

RATER HAS WRITTEN COMMENTS ELSEWHERE

Signature	Date

Set no. 0056488

Mark last 3 digits of Set number in area below.

:0:	:1:	:2:	:3:	:4:		:5:	:6:	:7:	:8:	:9:
:0:	:1:	:2:	:3:	:4:		:5:	:6:	:7:	:8:	:9:
:0:	:1:	:2:	:3:	:4:		:5:	:6:	:7:	:8:	:9:

IBM M62394

MSER 4b

Content Theme of hallucinations, including interpretation patient gives to hallucinations.
Conviction that hallucinations are real The extent to which patient is convinced that hallucinations are perceptions of real external events.
Illusions The misinterpretation or alteration of a real external sensory experience to be distinguished from hallucinations, e.g. chime of clock is heard as an insulting remark; wind is heard as someone calling name.
Depersonalization Feelings of strangeness or unreality about one's own body, e.g. feels outside of body or as if part of body does not belong to him.
Derealization Feelings of strangeness or unreality about one's surroundings, e.g. everything is dreamlike.
Deja vu A subjective feeling that an experience which is occurring for the first time has been experienced before.

SENSORIUM
Orientation disturbance
 Time Does not know the year, season, month, day, or time of day.
 Place Does not know where he is or in what kind of place he is.
 Person (self and others) Does not know who he is or misidentifies others.
Memory disturbance General disturbance in memory not limited to a discrete time period (as with hysterical amnesia).
 Recent Events of the last few hours or days.
 Remote Events of several years ago.
Clouding of consciousness Disturbance in perception, attention and thought with a subsequent amnesia.
 Fluctuating Intermittent returning to normal consciousness.
 Continuous No return to normal consciousness.
Dissociation A psychological separation or splitting off of behavior or events from consciousness.
 Trance Marked unresponsiveness to the environment, usually of sudden onset, with a degree of immobility and a dazed appearance.
 Amnesia A loss of memory for a circumscribed period of time on a psychological basis; to be distinguished from a generalized memory disturbance as above.
 Fugue A period of amnesia with physical flight from a stressful situation with retention of habits and skills.
 Hysterical attack Marked emotional display with a strong histrionic flavor and apparent loss of contact with the environment.
 Other Examples: somnambulism, automatic writing, Ganser syndrome.

COGNITIVE FUNCTIONS
Attention disturbance Inability to focus on one component of a situation. Impairment may be observed by the rater or be a subjective complaint of the patient.
Distractability Attention is too easily drawn to unimportant or irrelevant stimuli.

Intelligence (estimate) Takes into account native ingenuity as well as vocabulary, academic achievements and available IQ scores. **Superior:** IQ 120+, **Bright:** 110-119, **Average:** 90-109, **Borderline:** 70-89, **Retarded:** below 70.

JUDGMENT
Ability to evaluate alternative courses of action or to draw proper conclusions from experience.
 Family relations Immediate or extended family, e.g. doesn't appreciate how his behavior upsets family.
 Other social relations Example: Continually feels mistreated by strangers.
 Employment Example: Unrealistic job expectations.
 Future plans Note either that the patient has no plans, or note the level of judgment for plans that he does have.

POTENTIAL FOR SUICIDE OR VIOLENCE
Estimate of potential for behavior in the next few days, weeks, or month.

IBM M62395

INSIGHT — ATTITUDE TOWARD ILLNESS
Use the **not applicable** category for each item if the patient is not ill now. Use the **unknown** category if patient is ill but his insight or attitude cannot be ascertained, e.g. patient is mute.
Recognition that he is ill Realization that he has emotional, mental, or psychiatric problems or symptoms.
Motivation for working on problem in some realistic manner. May involve changing his life circumstances, attitudes, or behavior. Note whether the patient desires or refuses the treatment that is being offered.
Awareness of his contribution to difficulties Use **not applicable** if the nature of the difficulty appears to be due entirely to external influences, e.g. toxic psychosis because of febrile illness. Note if patient blames circumstances and/or other people for his difficulties.

OVERALL SEVERITY OF ILLNESS
during this one week study period. Consider all of the previous items and any other evidence of psychopathology. Do not include prognosis.

CHANGE IN CONDITION
Note the most appropriate descriptive term (e.g. marked improvement) for the past week.

RATER HAS WRITTEN COMMENTS ELSEWHERE
Note if additional comments about the patient's current condition have been recorded elsewhere in the clinical record.

Index

Index

About the Authors

William Getz, a member of the Academy of Certified Social Workers, received the M.S.W. from the University of Washington. He is Field Work Instructor in the School of Social Work and Affiliate Assistant Professor of Psychology at the University of Washington. He is also Program Director of the Crisis Intervention Service at Valley General Hospital and a consultant to the Criminal Justice Education Training Center. Mr. Getz maintains a private practice of psychotherapy in Bellevue, Washington.

Allen E. Wiesen received the Ph.D. from the University of Florida; he is engaged in private practice of clinical psychology in Bellevue, Washington. He was formerly affiliated with the Seattle Crisis Clinic and the Seattle Open Door Clinic. Dr. Wiesen is coauthor of *Changing Classroom Behavior* (Intext, 1969, 1974) and author of *A Police Officer's Guide to Crisis Intervention and Abnormal Behavior* (Braunstein, 1974).

Stan Sue received the Ph.D. from the University of California at Los Angeles. He is Assistant Professor of Psychology at the University of Washington and maintains a private practice in Seattle. Dr. Sue is coauthor of *Asian Americans: Psychological Perspectives* (Science and Behavior Books, 1973) and has contributed numerous articles to professional psychology and counseling journals.

Amy Ayers, R.N., is Psychiatric Nursing Supervisor at Overlake Memorial Hospital in Bellevue, Washington.